DEMOCRATIC DILEMMAS OF
TEACHING SERVICE-LEARNING

DEMOCRATIC DILEMMAS OF TEACHING SERVICE-LEARNING

Curricular Strategies for Success

Christine M. Cress,
David M. Donahue,
and Associates

Foreword by Thomas Ehrlich

1996–2011 15™ANNIVERSARY

Sty/us PUBLISHING, LLC.

STERLING, VIRGINIA

COPYRIGHT © 2011 BY STYLUS PUBLISHING, LLC.

Published by Stylus Publishing, LLC
22883 Quicksilver Drive
Sterling, Virginia 20166-2102

Library of Congress Cataloging-in-Publication-Data
Democratic dilemmas of teaching service-learning : curricular strategies for success / edited by Christine M. Cress and David M. Donahue ; foreword by Thomas Ehrlich.—1st ed.
    p.   cm.
Includes bibliographical references and index.
ISBN 978-1-57922-430-1 (cloth : alk. paper)
ISBN 978-1-57922-431-8 (pbk. : alk. paper)
ISBN 978-1-57922-599-5 (library networkable e-edition)
ISBN 978-1-57922-600-8 (consumer e-edition)
1. Service learning—Study and teaching (Higher)—United States.   2. Democracy and education—United States.
3. Critical pedagogy—United States.   I. Cress, Christine M. (Christine Marie), 1962–   II. Donahue, David M.
LC220.5.D46   2011
378.1'03—dc22

                                        2010044688

13-digit ISBN: 978-1-57922-430-1 (cloth)
13-digit ISBN: 978-1-57922-431-8 (paper)
13-digit ISBN: 978-1-57922-599-5 (library networkable e-edition)
13-digit ISBN: 978-1-57922-600-8 (consumer e-edition)

Printed in the United States of America

All first editions printed on acid free paper that meets the American National Standards Institute Z39-48 Standard.

Bulk Purchases

Quantity discounts are available for use in workshops and for staff development.
Call 1-800-232-0223

First Edition, 2011

10   9   8   7   6   5   4   3   2

In appreciation for
Ann and Vern
Mary and John

CONTENTS

PART FIVE: ACADEMIC DISCIPLINES AS DIMENSIONS OF DEMOCRACY

PART SIX: EVALUATING DEMOCRATIC PROCESS AND PROGRESS

In the late 1920s and 1930s, freshmen at Stanford University were required to take a yearlong course called "Problems of Citizenship." The course was one-fourth of the normal first-year undergraduate curriculum; it was rooted in the judgments of the University's founders, Jane and Leland Stanford, that education for civic leadership should be a primary goal of an undergraduate education. In the words of Mrs. Stanford, "While the instruction offered must be such as will qualify the students for personal success and direct usefulness in life, they should understand that it is offered in the hope and trust that they will become thereby of greater service to the public." The course was designed by members of a faculty committee who based their design on the conviction that "freshmen are destined to become leaders in their respective communities. [At Stanford] they are forming the political and economic and social ideas that will characterize that leadership." *

In the opening lecture in 1928, the first year the course was offered, Professor Edgar Eugene Robinson told students that

Citizenship is the second calling of every man and woman. You will observe as we go forward that our constant endeavor will be to relate what we do and say to the facts of the world from which you came and in which all of you will live, and to correlate the various aspects of the modern scene, so that it will appear that citizenship is not a thing apart, something to be thought of only occasionally or left to the energies of a minority of our people, but that its proper understanding is at the very root of our daily life.

What a contrast was this course, and others like it that were taught at colleges and universities around the country in the first half of the twentieth

---

* The story of the Stanford course on Problems of Citizenship and the related quotations are based on Chapter VI in the wonderful little volume by W. B. Carnochan, *The Battleground of the Curriculum* (Stanford University Press, Stanford, CA, 1993). Professor Robinson's first lecture in the course is reproduced in the appendix.

century, with most contemporary courses in political science today, courses in which students learn about governments and their activities, but not about how—as responsible citizens—to engage in those activities and to influence them. So what happened? A number of forces led to the shifts, but one was particularly important. In the post World War II years, disinterested, disengaged analysis became the dominant mode of academic inquiry, and quantitative methods became the primary tools of that analysis. Students were no longer encouraged to become actively engaged in making democracy work. They were educated to be observers, not participants.

This perspective had a powerful effect not just on college students, but on the teaching of what had been called civics in secondary schools. A primary aim of high-school civics courses in the era before World War II had been to prepare young students to be actively engaged, responsible civic leaders in their communities, involved in politics at every level. The new trend drained the civics courses of their activist aims. Learning about government was substituted for participating in it, as logical positivism became the mantra in American higher education, not just in the sciences, but in the social sciences as well.

Fortunately, over recent decades, there has been renewed attention to integrating academic learning with learning for active, engaged citizenship. A number of forces have been at work, including Campus Compact, the Corporation for National and Community Service (and its predecessor, the Commission on National and Community Service), and the Corporation's program, called "Learn & Serve," which is dedicated to promoting service-learning at colleges and universities across the country. Today it is hard to find a campus in the United States where community service-learning is not a major part of undergraduate education. By community service-learning I mean linking academic study and civic work through structured reflection. Scores of books have been written about that pedagogy and other forms of educating for civic engagement. High-school students applying to American colleges these days know that they should mention their civic work—and many high schools require that work as a condition of graduation.

There are exceptions. Some years ago, I participated in a public forum at the American Academy of Arts and Sciences. The issue was whether community service-learning is a sound pedagogy for undergraduates, as I have strongly urged. Harvard Law School professor Charles Fried, former Solicitor General of the United States, was among the panelists, and he objected to my approach. During the undergraduate years, he said, there should be a "moratorium" on student interactions with society. Young people in those years, he argued, should "be confronted with ideas, with truths, with reflection somewhat detached, perhaps even entirely detached, from the practical consequences of what they are learning." Undergraduates will be "submerged in practical consequences for the whole rest of their lives." College years are a time to learn "things that are to be understood for their own sake, understood for the truths they contain."

Some college faculty would be pleased with Fried's "moratorium." They may find it threatening that students might learn outside the classroom and apply that learning to enrich their academic learning—that they might learn something that the faculty member does not know. They may claim, like Fried, that undergraduates should look solely inward, enriched by great minds and their great books. But they fail to recognize the compelling evidence that service-learning actually enhances academic learning in the humanities, the social and natural sciences, and in vocational fields. Precisely because it is a relatively new pedagogy, and was met with faculty skepticism, service-learning has been the subject of more research than any other pedagogy over the last decades. Research has given powerful evidence that service learning and other pedagogies that promote civic engagement also increase both college access and success, as "A Promising Connection," the monograph published by Campus Compact, makes clear.

The approach that Robinson adopted in the Stanford course drew on the work of John Dewey among others. In his great book, *Education and Democracy*, Dewey argued that our democracy requires an engaged citizenry to realize the potential of its citizens and its civic leaders. Dewey did not give concrete examples or even many hints about how best to promote civic responsibility in our students. He was never one to practice what he preached—a failing of many in higher education. As was so often the case, he suggested a framework and left the details to others. But it is clear that he believed a school should be a microcosm of society, structured in ways that enhance the learning environment by simplifying and organizing. He stressed two key "conditions" (as he called them). First, the school must itself mirror community life, in all that implies. Second, the learning in school should be continuous with that outside the classroom.

Dewey had two radical insights about U.S society. One was that most citizens, not just an elite, can have a life of the mind. The other was that a life that is only of the mind is inadequate to the challenges of American democracy. Our society requires civic engagement to realize the potential of its citizens and its civic leaders. Dewey did not give concrete examples or even many hints about how best to promote civic responsibility in our students. He did, however, stress three key elements in the democratic learning process. First, that process should engage students in reaching outside the walls of the school and into the surrounding community; second, it should focus on problems to be solved; and third, it should be collaborative, both among students and between students and faculty.

Each of these elements is reflected in an active pedagogy—a pedagogy of engagement—that is increasingly infusing undergraduate education throughout the country. First, community service-learning, to supplement closed classroom learning; second, problem-based learning, in addition to discipline-based learning; and third, collaborative learning, as well as individual learning. These are not the only pedagogic strategies for civic education, but on the basis of my work over the past decades they seem to me particularly promising for realizing Dewey's ideas and ideals. They also underscore that how a subject is taught is as important as what is taught.

Each of the three pedagogies is clearly visible in the splendid essays that make up this impressive volume. It is a significant contribution to a steadily growing body of scholarly work on educating for political engagement. Common to these strategies are two threads that spiral through them like a double helix. Education as a social and socializing function is the first. For Dewey, education must be both an individual function and a community function; the two were interdependent. The one motivated students to learn; the other made that learning worthwhile. Attention solely on the individual without community leads to self-indulgence and to the privatization and atomization of learning; focus on the community without attention to the individual tends toward conformity, coercion, and even stagnation.

The second common thread is a shift from teaching to learning and a shift in the role of faculty member from teacher to coach and mentor, as described by the scholars who wrote essays in this volume. The thread marks a return to Dewey's concept that student interest should be the starting point in education. Of all elements in Dewey's views on education, this can be the most easily misunderstood, for it sounds suspiciously like a call to let students play in sandboxes or do whatever else they want to do. Instead, it was a call to shape learning experiences around the individual interests and needs of students.

Anne Colby, my former colleague at the Carnegie Foundation for the Advancement of Teaching, and I are pleased that we had dual roles in helping to build a foundation on which the book takes important strides forward. First, we were co-authors of two earlier works, *Educating Citizens: Preparing America's Undergraduates for Lives of Moral and Civic Responsibility* (Jossey-Bass, 2003) and *Educating for Democracy: Preparing Undergraduates for Responsible Political Engagement* (Jossey-Bass, 2007) that provide some of the basis on which this volume builds. Particularly in the second book, we explored ways in which colleges and universities can best ensure that their students graduate with the knowledge, skills, and attitudes to be responsible participants in politics, by which we include all aspects of public policy-making. Second, Anne and I participated in a program sponsored by California Campus Compact, that brought together faculty from a number of different disciplines to reshape existing courses and to develop new ones to make educating for political engagement integral to their students' learning. Most of the essays in this volume are written by faculty who participated in that program. Anne and I were enormously impressed over the course of the program by the ways in which a brilliant and motivated group of faculty members from a diverse set of California campuses infused education for political engagement in a wide range of different disciplinary and interdisciplinary courses targeted at a diverse groups of students.

A central tenet of both our earlier works, one that is particularly addressed in *Educating for Democracy*, is what we term the imperative of open inquiry. College campuses are among the few venues these days that are not conducive to the cross-fire approach that so dominates public discussions of many political issues, particularly the hot-button kind. Open inquiry should be a core value of the academy, and this means that courses must be taught in ways that do not promote the ideological biases of the faculty teaching them. In *Educating for Democracy*, we studied 21 courses and programs that seemed to do a particularly good job of the kind of instruction we were championing. We surveyed students at the beginning and end of these courses and programs and found not only that the students gained in terms of the knowledge, skills, and motivations that we had identified, but they did not shift in their own ideological positions from liberal to conservative or the reverse.

This volume takes as its starting point that what the editors term "democratic dilemmas" can be particularly powerful tools in teaching for political engagement. As a way to underscore the potential in using such dilemmas, they begin with the hypothetical of a college student who "wants to lead a campaign to ban a young adult novel from his child's elementary school as his service-learning project in a children's literature course." The example is a terrific one, because it underscores precisely the imperative of open inquiry that Anne and I believe is so important. In the essays that follow, the authors examine how almost two dozen faculty members in a range of disciplines use actual dilemmas to come directly to grips with democracy and its complexities. They do so with wisdom and insights that will be useful to faculty in a wide range of institutions and disciplines.

Over the course of recent decades, I have been increasingly concerned by the evidence that our democracy is in serious trouble. College students are not alone responsible for fixing the messes that the generations before them have created. But unless they are educated to engage in democracy—and not simply sit on the sidelines—the mess can only get worse—much worse. This book is a powerful set of lessons about how to engage college students in ways that are challenging, provocative, and most important, that provide learning that lasts for active citizenry. I cannot imagine a more important task.

Thomas Ehrlich
Visiting professor at the school of
education, Stanford University, and
former president of Indiana University

COMPETING DEMOCRATIC VALUES IN TEACHING AND LEARNING

Christine M. Cress and David M. Donahue

A college student wants to lead a campaign to ban a young adult novel from his child's elementary school as his service-learning project in a children's literature course. Believing the book is offensive to religious sensibilities, he sees his campaign as a service to children and the community. Viewing such a ban as limiting freedom of speech and access to information, the student's professor questions whether leading a ban qualifies as a service project. If the goal of service is to promote more vital democratic communities, what should the student do? What should the professor do? How do they untangle competing democratic values? How do they make a decision about action?

Dilemmas in Service-Learning

Colby, Beaumont, Ehrlich, and Corngold (2007) and others (Battistoni, 1997; Eyler & Giles, 1999; Jacoby & Associates, 2003; Mann & Patrick, 2000) have promoted the vehicle of service-learning as an important educational and pedagogical strategy for teaching students democratic values, principles, and practices. For those unfamiliar with the nature of service-learning, service-learning courses are classes specifically designed to engage students in community service activities with intentional learning objectives and opportunities for reflective integration that connect to students' academic disciplines (Cress, Collier, Reitenauer, & Associates 2005). The goal is to produce critically, civically, and globally minded graduates who possess problem-solving and leadership abilities for more socially equitable and sustainable communities as a part of healthy, functioning democratic societies (Colby, Ehrlich, Beaumont, & Stephens, 2003).

Conflicts among freedom of religion, freedom from discrimination, freedom of political choice, free press, and free speech are just some of the myriad democratic dilemmas that faculty face while teaching service-learning. Cuban (2001) describes dilemmas as complicated, interconnected situations where competing values create tensions and potential conflict with no single correct response or action. Individuals dealing with a dilemma are compelled to compromise and bargain across their own competing values often sacrificing deeply held principles in an attempt to find common ground.

This book highlights actual teaching dilemmas, like the one at the beginning of this introduction, where instructors and students have grappled with the democratic tensions and trials of learning and identified pedagogical and epistemological responses to meet those challenges. The text navigates the reader through the hurdles of teaching service-learning courses by addressing questions of democratic meaning and values as, for example, faculty and students address the potential irony of "requiring" democratic engagement and struggle with the essence of what it means to be a learner, a citizen, and a community member as part of micro and macro democratic processes.

Pedagogical Strategies

Nearly two dozen faculty scholars from diverse disciplines including computer science, engineering, English, history, and sociology take readers on their and their students' intellectual journeys, sharing their messy, unpredictable, and often inspiring accounts of democratic tensions and trials inherent in teaching service-learning. Using real incidents, resources, and classroom activities, they explore the democratic intersections of various political beliefs along with race/ethnicity, class, gender, ability, sexual orientation, and other lived differences and likenesses that students and faculty experience in their service-learning classroom and extended community. They share their struggles of how to communicate and interact across the divide of viewpoints and experiences within an egalitarian and inclusive environment all the while managing interpersonal tensions and conflicts among diverse people in complex, value-laden situations.

As Dewey (1916) noted, democracy is more than voting or accepting jury duty. It is a *mode of associated living* where communities of people representing diverse perspectives engage in dialogue and decision making. The faculty authors in *Democratic Dilemmas* illustrate how they and their students respond to the dilemmas inherent in any community of diverse individuals making decisions with political implications, whether those implications are about who talks, who is heard, and who decides. In short, readers will come to understand that teaching service-learning is not merely educating for democracy, but practicing it as well.

The Purpose of *Democratic Dilemmas*

With the call for a service nation by President Barack Obama, there has never been a more catalytic time for a book like *Democratic Dilemmas*. Colleges and universities have long claimed a role in educating young people for democracy, but many faculty remain unclear or conflicted about how to do so in ways that are academically rigorous and scrupulously unbiased.

Democratic Dilemmas fits into—and is needed in—a world where service-learning as a pedagogy is prevalent, and where vast national dollars are dedicated not only to sustaining but to advancing the implementation of service-learning throughout higher education. Currently, more than 630 public and private 2- and 4-year colleges and universities implement service-learning on their campuses, and each year students enrolled at Campus Compact–member institutions provide more than 22 million hours of community service. In addition, the Corporation for National and Community Service has distributed $10 million in funding over the last three years to colleges and universities that have implemented innovative service-learning programs in which 30,000 students have participated.

Democratic Dilemmas complements two other books on preparing college students for political engagement: *Educating for Democracy: Preparing Undergraduates for Responsible Political Engagement* (Colby et al., 2007) and *Research, Advocacy, and Political Engagement: Multidisciplinary Perspectives Through Service Learning* (Tannenbaum, 2008). The first book, *Educating for Democracy*, calls forth the need for service-learning for political engagement, presenting well-reasoned arguments for the importance of educating for democratic participation and offering practical and much-needed guidelines for faculty and administrators who want to help their students become more fully engaged in political life. The second book, *Research, Advocacy, and Political Engagement*, features a compilation of presentations by California State University faculty members from diverse disciplines on how they have used service-learning to introduce students to political engagement. The faculty authors explain their objectives and provide course syllabi and assessments of outcomes.

Democratic Dilemmas takes the subject of service-learning a step further—with scholars reflecting on how their courses and community experiences shape students' opportunities to make democratic meaning of their service, the implications of students' actual learning for promoting deeper understanding of political engagement, and an increased disposition to engage in democratic processes inside and outside the classroom.

The chapters in *Democratic Dilemmas* are teaching cases in the purest, most comprehensive sense—they do not necessarily end neatly; the work is complicated and fraught with disagreements and differences. Moreover, unique to this book is how academic disciplinary analysis is applied to each of the dilemmas central to the teaching cases. Democratic dilemmas are framed, problematized, and addressed through the research and literature of each author's academic field. As such, the learning opportunities for the faculty and students who have lived the dilemmas as well as the reader experiencing the story through its retelling are rigorous and academically grounded, offering specific pedagogical strategies for the success of future service-learning courses.

Organizationally, each teaching case study chapter begins with contextual and logistical information about the course and then outlines the democratic dilemmas faced by the instructor and students. Names of individuals and organizations have been changed for the purpose of anonymity. If necessary, some elements of the actual situations have been deleted to protect confidentiality. In other cases, limited fictionalized prose has been added to highlight key concepts or assist with reading flow and transition. However, all the teaching chapters are based on real events and democratic dilemmas faced by the service-learning instructors. So, most importantly, the creative ideas and strategies for turning these dilemmas into teaching and learning opportunities come directly from the expertise and wisdom of the chapters' authors.

Contributing Authors and Organizational Support

The majority of authors were part of a collaboration of the Carnegie Foundation for the Advancement of Teaching and Learning and California Campus Compact funded by the Corporation for National and Community Service as part of a Learn and Serve America Higher Education Grant. With participants selected as Faculty Fellows, the program focused on service-learning for political engagement. California Campus Compact provided organizational and grant support for the Fellows with the intellectual guidance and expertise of Tom Ehrlich and Anne Colby, senior scholars in Carnegie's Political Engagement Project.

The Faculty Fellows, from a wide array of private and public colleges and universities, participated in two intensive service-learning summer institutes in 2007 and 2008 at the Carnegie Foundation and as part of an ongoing Fellows learning community that was facilitated by us, Christine M. Cress and David M. Donahue. Faculty Fellows drew from the insights of experts in the service-learning field and shared with one another their ideas, strategies, and encouragement about how to negotiate their service-learning classrooms, community organizations, institutional structures, and disciplinary scholarly norms and expectations.

Over the course of the fellows program, one pedagogical element continued to surface: strategies for framing and responding to inevitable tensions and conflicts resulting from an explicit focus on the political dimension of service. Overlaying the pedagogical considerations was a continued discussion and examination of teaching and learning generally and service-learning specifically as democratic processes and how such efforts could be conducted through nonpartisan political engagement. Faculty shared teaching strategies along with insights from successes and challenges faced by students, community members, and the instructors themselves.

While not an official publication of California Campus Compact or the Carnegie Foundation for the Advancement of Teaching and Learning, this book would not be possible without their collaborative efforts that resulted in the Faculty Fellows Program in Service-Learning for Political Engagement.

About California Campus Compact

Since its founding in 1988, California Campus Compact has worked to build the collective commitment and capacity of colleges, universities, and communities throughout California to advance civic and community engagement for a healthy, just, and democratic society. Through innovative programs and initiatives, grant funding, training and technical assistance, professional development, and powerful research studies and publications, California Campus Compact each year invests in and champions more than 500,000 students, faculty members, administrators, and community members involved in diverse and groundbreaking activities that support and expand civic and community engagement throughout California.

About the Carnegie Foundation for the Advancement of Teaching and Learning

Founded by Andrew Carnegie in 1905 and chartered in 1906 by an act of Congress, The Carnegie Foundation for the Advancement of Teaching is an independent policy and research center whose charge is "to do and perform all things necessary to encourage, uphold, and dignify the profession of the teacher." The improvement of teaching and learning is central to all the foundation's work. It brings together researchers, teachers, policy makers, and members of organizations with common interests in education, and works to invent new knowledge and to develop tools and ideas that allow educators to foster positive change and enhanced learning in our nation's schools.

The Terminology of Service-Learning

Service-learning is a unique pedagogical approach to teaching and learning that strategically combines academic concepts, community service, and active reflection. The purpose of service-learning is to enrich understanding of academic discipline knowledge while building skill sets for applying this knowledge to real-life community challenges. The overarching goal of service-learning is to prepare students for engaged lives as members of their democratic communities with insights and abilities about how to effectively contribute to and improve their neighborhoods and cities. Ultimately, such experiences should also lead to students' understanding how their individual actions can have not only a local but also a national and global impact.

Use of the term *service-learning* varies widely across educational systems and organizations. Some colleges favor the term *community-based learning*. Other postsecondary organizations and institutions focus on *community engagement* or *civic engagement* as a way to define learning linkages between classrooms and communities. For the purposes of *Democratic Dilemmas*, we have embraced service-learning as the phrase most generally applicable to the teaching and learning dilemmas faced by faculty and students in trying to create engaged democratic communities of academic practice inside and outside the classroom. Moreover, since many of the contributors participated in the California Campus Compact Faculty Fellows for Political Engagement project in collaboration with The Carnegie Foundation for the Advancement of Teaching and Learning, this book echoes the assertion of Colby et al. (2007) that those in higher education have a responsibility to educate for democracy in preparing students for responsible political engagement.

That said, the teaching case chapters that illustrate the service-learning democratic dilemmas are framed using terminology specific to each contributor's own institution and course. This approach captures the language and structure of the disciplines along with the nuances of the particular college or university and the wide variety of academic programs and community engagement approaches. It allows readers to embed themselves in the full context of democratic teaching dilemmas and thereby draw relevant applications for courses at their own institutions.

We offer two caveats regarding the contents of the book. First, with one exception, all the teaching cases take place in the United States. As such, cultural and community differences are generally defined and described in the context of U.S. values and norms. Certainly, hundreds of colleges have long participated in international student and faculty exchange programs, and scores of higher education institutions have begun to develop international service-learning programs. Second, nearly all the teaching cases involve undergraduate students. Again, many colleges and universities have extended service-learning into graduate and professional programs including Portland State University, which now has a master's degree specialization and graduate certificate in service-learning and community-based learning (see http://www.pdx.edu/elp/service-learning). Still, the pedagogical content and the teaching case chapters are broad enough to apply to any educational or discipline setting while offering specific strategies and ideas for effective service-learning.

Section and Chapter Overview of *Democratic Dilemmas*

Part One, "Democratic Dilemmas of Teaching Service-Learning," outlines the challenges and opportunities inherent in teaching course content through community engagement. In the first chapter, "The Nature of Teaching and Learning Dilemmas: Democracy in the Making," David M. Donahue outlines and defines the explicit and implicit value conflicts that emerge in any teaching endeavor that can become even more challenging when the venue for learning involves the community outside the classroom.

In Chapter 2, "Banning Books to Protect Children: Clashing Perspectives in Service-Learning," Lynne A. Bercaw illustrates real-life democratic dilemmas of freedom of the press, freedom of speech, and freedom of choice for students and faculty alike. Bercaw describes the clash between democratic teaching ideals and the promotion of student autonomy in learning and behavior.

Similarly, Caroline Heldman, in Chapter 3, "Solidarity, Not Charity: Issues of Privilege in Service-Learning," examines how student service in New Orleans after Hurricane Katrina challenges students' sense of identity as individual citizens with collective responsibility for rectifying community social and economic inequities. She describes how unexamined privilege in service can reinforce elitist stereotypes.

Part Two, "Designing Service-Learning Courses for Democratic Outcomes," offers the reader pedagogical strategies for managing democratic conflicts through intentional service-learning course structure and design. Chapter 4, "Pedagogical and Epistemological Approaches to Service-Learning: Connecting Academic Content to Community Service," by Christine M. Cress, offers a step-by-step approach for designing course syllabi to help ensure explicit academic connections to civic engagement.

One strategy by Dari E. Sylvester in Chapter 5, "Student Objection to Service-Learning: A Teachable Moment About Political and Community Engagement," for overcoming student resistance to service-learning is to encourage students who have engaged in civic engagement previously to share their positive experiences with classmates even though service-learning can raise feelings of fear and inferiority in students about how to address community challenges.

Indeed, Katja M. Guenther, in Chapter 6, "Practice Makes Imperfect: Service-Learning for Political Engagement as a Window Into the Challenges of Political Organizing," argues that a fundamental reason for requiring service-learning is to give students insight into the complexities of society and social change. Essentially, students need democratic practice in addition to conceptual principles.

Although, as Stephanie Stokamer points out in Chapter 7, "Modeling Citizenship: The Nexus of Knowledge and Skill," teaching citizenship through service-learning can initially make students feel overwhelmed and disempowered by the myriad complexities of social inequalities. Faculty must therefore critically attend to civic skill and civic knowledge development in their pedagogical preparation if students are to become democratically empowered through service-learning.

Part Three, "Creating Democratic Learning Communities Within and Without," further examines how to create democratic communities of learners within the classroom and through collaborations with community organizations and agencies.

Christine M. Cress in Chapter 8, "Consensus, Collaboration, and Community: Mutually Exclusive Ideals?" discusses how to develop effective college–community connections for enhanced student learning and community improvement.

Judith Liu in Chapter 9, "Cultivating Relationships Between a Grassroots Organization and a University," relates the logistical and value-laden challenges of establishing common expectations and responsibilities when negotiating a service-learning relationship with a community organization.

In turn, Marcia Hernandez in Chapter 10, "Negotiating Student Expectations and Interpretations of Service-Learning," conveys students' narrow perceptions of community agencies and shows how paradoxically those students initially with the most negative views of one community organization actually gained the most knowledge and skill from their service-learning.

Addressing and helping students adjust their paradigmatic cultural frames of reference is the focus of Chapter 11, "Service-Learning Is Like Learning to Walk: Baby Steps to Cultural Competence," by Tanya Renner, RaeLyn Axlund, Lucero Topete, and Molli K. Fleming. The authors describe an international service-learning experience fraught with student, faculty, and community differences in roles and expectations but ultimately fruitful in its learning and service impact.

In Part Four, "Deconstructing Dilemmas for Democratically Centered Learning," conflict in service-learning is acknowledged as inevitable, but also as serving an important pedagogical purpose.

David M. Donahue in Chapter 12, "Conflict as a Constructive Curricular Strategy," details multiple teaching strategies for negotiating the learning terrain of conflict.

Kathleen S. Yep in Chapter 13, "Why Are You So Mad? Critical Multi-culturalist Pedagogies and Mediating Racial Conflicts in Community-Based Learning," depicts a dreaded fear for most instructors—dealing with a self-proclaimed student outcast whose comments and behaviors, whether in ignorance or mean-spiritedness, raise the ire of the entire classroom community. In this case, the professor has to strategize how to minimize the impact on the class as well as the community while continuing to facilitate the learning trajectory of the student.

Becky Boesch grapples with some of the same issues in Chapter 14, "Working With High School Dropouts: Service-Learning Illustrations of Power and Privilege." Her students, many of whom are first-generation college students, turn on their GED mentees and blame them for their academic failures. Boesch describes strategies to help college students see larger social, economic, and educational systems that affect high school retention and graduation.

Understanding multiple perspectives is the purpose of democratic education that Thomas J. Van Cleave describes in Chapter 15, "Democratic Lessons in Faith, Service, and Sexuality." He wrestles with how to support a student with strong religious beliefs who feels victimized by his liberal classmates and resists service-learning at an HIV/AIDS hospice. As Van Cleave writes on p. 127, "Perhaps . . . the greatest democratic lesson we can offer our students through service-learning [is] feeling comfortable in the dissonance of difference."

Part Five, "Academic Disciplines as Dimensions of Democracy," explores how the paradigmatic lenses of academic disciplines can be used to investigate, analyze, and problem solve the complexities of community challenges and attendant democratic dilemmas.

In Chapter 16, "Disciplinary Knowledge, Service-Learning, and Citizenship," David M. Donahue analyzes how disciplinary knowledge can move beyond theoretical examinations to leveraging solutions for change and supporting critical thinking processes that foster critical consciousness and action.

Academic discipline–based strategies for engaging students in active citizenship participation are addressed by Christopher Brooks in Chapter 17, "Why Should I Care? Introducing Service-Learning and Political Engagement to Computer Science Students," and Corey Cook in Chapter 18, "Political Science Students and the Disengaged Polis: Civic Education and

Its Discontents." Brooks describes instructional techniques for creating connections between the community and skeptical (even resistant) students, some of whom selected a major with a technology focus because they did not want to be involved in dilemmas of social inequalities. Brooks relates how to bridge digital divides in and outside the classroom.

Cook's political science students, in contrast, begin their service-learning eagerly through civic education of ballot measures. To their disappointment, the polis appears uninterested. Cook articulates the democratic dilemmas in the community concerning voter participation, his students' work to grapple with civic education versus voting advocacy, and his own roles as a teacher in reframing reactions as teachable political science moments.

Sandra A. Sgoutas-Emch in Chapter 19, "Health Psychology and Political Engagement: The Why and How," further illustrates how student perceptions of academic disciplines (in this case, psychology) are often limited to content readings and research rather than construed as professional forums for future impact. By intentionally redesigning her service-learning course to have a political engagement emphasis, her students come to understand themselves as psychology professionals who can have an impact on political processes and policies for the greater health of communities.

In Chapter 20, "To Reform or to Empower? Asian American Studies and Education for Critical Consciousness," Kathleen S. Yep shows how becoming active citizens is inextricably bound with interrogating power and privilege in theory and practice and how Asian American studies can be a vehicle for creating democratic learning environments and solidarity in community-based learning. After classroom tensions erupt concerning service work with incarcerated youth, Yep uses an Asian American studies mapping exercise for understanding social locations and identifying sources of individual agency to overcome student feelings of being overwhelmed by the complexities of racial discrimination and other social injustices.

Part Six, "Evaluating Democratic Process and Progress," identifies strategies and approaches for assessing democracy in the making, whether developing the democratic knowledge, skills, and attitudes of individual students or using research methodologies to collect community data in trying to influence positive change.

In Chapter 21, "Assessment of Expected and Unexpected Service-Learning Outcomes," Christine M. Cress offers a theoretical approach to assessing service-learning processes and outcomes and describes specific quantitative and qualitative techniques that can be applied to various methodological designs.

Catherine Gabor in Chapter 22, "Expecting the Political, Getting the Interview: How Students (Do Not) See Writing as a Political Act," wants students to see her professional writing course as a form of political action where writing is not divorced from the real world. She discusses how qualitative data, through focus groups and interviews, gave her insights for course redesign in creating intersections among writing, service-learning, and political engagement.

Effective use of quantitative and qualitative data is described by Laura Nichols, Fernando Cázares, and Angelica Rodriguez in Chapter 23, "Addressing Policy Dilemmas With Community-Based Research and Assessing Student Outcomes." Approaches are outlined regarding sociology students who collect community-based research data on homeless individuals who ride public buses for shelter. The data become critical components for community discussion as collaborating agencies get new views on the issues and potential solutions. In addition, data on the service-learning students themselves indicate increased political efficacy as a result of the course project.

Finally, "Service-Learning for a Democratic Future," Chapter 24, by David M. Donahue and Christine M. Cress, summarizes and rehighlights the key pedagogical approaches and practices from the contributors and offers additional ideas and strategies for future teaching, research, and scholarship.

The generous and authentic sharing of the contributors' struggles and insights offer readers of *Democratic Dilemmas of Teaching Service-Learning* the opportunity to become engaged, inspired, and ultimately to find themselves with multiple new curricular strategies for service-learning success. Our special thanks and indebted gratitude to Elaine Ikeda and Piper McGinley at California Campus Compact, and Tom Ehrlich and Anne Colby at The Carnegie Foundation for the Advancement of Teaching and Learning, without whom the Faculty Fellows for Political Engagement project would not have been possible. As well, to our wonderful author colleagues who willingly shared their democratic teaching dilemmas and marvelous pedagogical insights and ideas.

References

Battistoni, R. M. (1997). Service learning and democratic citizenship. *Theory Into Practice, 36*(3), 150–156.

Colby, A., Beaumont, E., Ehrlich, T., & Corngold, J. (2007). *Educating for democracy: Preparing undergraduates for responsible political engagement.* San Francisco: Jossey-Bass.

Colby, A., Ehrlich, T., Beaumont, E., & Stephens, J. (2003). *Educating citizens: Preparing America's undergraduates for lives of moral and civic responsibility.* San Francisco, CA: Jossey-Bass.

Cress, C. M., Collier, P. J., Reitenauer, V. L., & Associates. (2005). *Learning through serving: A student guidebook for service-learning across the disciplines.* Sterling, VA: Stylus.

Cuban, L. (2001). *Oversold and underused: Computers in the classroom.* Cambridge, MA: Harvard University Press.

Dewey, J. (1916). *Democracy and education.* New York, NY: The Free Press.

Eyler, J., & Giles, D. E., Jr. (1999). *Where's the learning in service-learning?* San Francisco, CA: Jossey-Bass.

Jacoby, B., & Associates (Eds.). (2003). *Building partnerships for service-learning.* San Francisco, CA: Jossey-Bass.

Mann, S., & Patrick, J. J. (Eds.). (2000). *Education for civic engagement in democracy.* Bloomington, IN: Education Resource Information Center.

Tannenbaum, S. C. (Ed.). (2008). *Research, advocacy, and political engagement: Multidisciplinary perspectives through service learning.* Sterling, VA: Stylus.

PART ONE

DEMOCRATIC DILEMMAS OF TEACHING SERVICE-LEARNING

THE NATURE OF TEACHING AND LEARNING DILEMMAS

Democracy in the Making

David M. Donahue

Teaching is an uncertain profession with innumerable questions. What do I want my students to know? Why do I think this is important? How will I know if they learned it? How will I know if their learning makes any difference in how they live their lives? Many of these questions are value laden and come with no single right answer. Consequently, teachers find they are navigating competing cultural, moral, and political values in the classroom. These competing values present dilemmas that are inherent in teaching.

Similarly, democratic political life is equally uncertain, and the questions are just as numerous. Who is a citizen? What are the rights of a citizen? How do we protect some people's rights without abridging the rights of others? How do we make decisions in a democratic society? These questions too are value laden, and the answers are not simple or singular. Participants in democratic life must also navigate dilemmas among competing values with cultural, moral, and political dimensions. These dilemmas are not obstacles or problems of democracy. They are the nature of democracy itself.

How then do college and university faculty prepare students for the uncertainties and dilemmas of political life given the uncertainties and dilemmas of classrooms? Does teaching to prepare students for engaging in political life multiply the dilemmas and uncertainties? If so, how is an instructor ever to meet this challenge?

When instructors make the uncertainties and dilemmas of teaching for political engagement explicit to themselves and their students, they create opportunities for learning about democratic political life that are rich, meaningful, and authentic. Dewey (1904) reminds us that education is not preparation for life, it is life itself. Consequently, by addressing the dilemmas of teaching for political engagement in the classrooms where they are situated, educators are engaging in the very life of democratic political communities they want students to engage in.

This chapter explains what the word *dilemma* means and why it is used to indicate a particular kind of pedagogical and political challenge. The chapter also describes why teaching in general and service-learning in particular are inherently political and how the inherently political nature of teaching and service-learning creates dilemmas for educators and students. Finally, dilemmas are described as framing a vital and productive part of the process of teaching and learning for political engagement through service-learning.

Dilemmas, Not Problems, of Teaching

It might not be an official part of the job description, but most teachers consider themselves problem solvers. Eighty-five students in a class a teacher thought might attract 40? Find a bigger room and no problem. The bookstore lost the order and none of the readings are available for the first class? Switch to plan B—lecture and discussion. The books arrive but fewer than half the students do the reading anyway? Require students to post blogs on at least half the texts to prompt them to read.

Teachers are capable problem solvers, but some problems of classroom life are not so easily resolved. What to do with the student who completes all assigned reading, shows up for every class, makes insightful observations in discussion, and bombs every quiz and the final? Should students' difficulties with writing at the college level mean dropping some written assignments from a course, revising standards for grading, or including intensive writing instruction? Do the sexist assumptions behind a student's comment in class present a teachable moment, a call for a reprimand, or a reason for wanting to limit this student's contributions?

As these situations illustrate, some problems are complex and without a single correct technical solution. Cuban (2001) describes these problems as dilemmas, noting they present "competing prized values" that result in "unattractive choices due to constraints" (p. 12) that require compromise. Ultimately, dilemmas are managed, not solved. When problems are solved, they go away. By contrast, faculty can respond to dilemmas, but they never go away. Instructors' responses allow them to move forward, but the tension among values still exists, and the responses may also result in new dilemmas farther down the road.

According to Cuban (2001), responding to dilemmas requires acknowledging their value-laden nature, framing them in a way that avoids blame, and balancing the competing values in the end. Acknowledging the value-laden nature of teaching dilemmas is not hard. Most often when faculty wrestle with these dilemmas, they ask what they should do, implying a normative rather than a technical question. Framing dilemmas without blame can be more challenging. Think about these scenarios. Perhaps a professor drives home from campus beating himself up for not anticipating all the difficulties that popped up in that day's class. Teachers can be hard on themselves because their expectations are high. Or perhaps that professor drove home wondering what was wrong with his students. Why didn't they understand some of the key concepts he was trying to teach? When teachers are frustrated, they can be hard on students. It's not easy to frame a disappointing class in terms of avoiding blame. Mismatched expectations about higher education, differing perspectives on the subject matter, or varied notions of what it means to discuss, for example, might help this professor see the failed class in a way that does not require assigning blame.

As difficult as it is to frame without blame, balancing competing values can be even more difficult. Consider the example of a student making a sexist comment in class. The instructor in this class might value a space where all can express their ideas however unpopular, an environment that is safe for all the diverse students in the class, and a forum where people are respected. The same instructor may want to encourage students to consider unpopular points of view, hear from students who might participate infrequently, and challenge the assumptions behind all students' thinking. Clearly, these are not easily balanced. Indeed, some values are contradictory. Cuban (2001) calls this balancing act "satisficing," or satisfying by sacrificing (p. 12).

Dilemmas, Not Problems, of Democracy

Problems of Democracy is the title of a civics or government course at many U.S. high schools. At the college level, political science courses may present students with opportunities to examine and propose policies to deal with public problems. But even seeming problems in a democracy can quickly turn to dilemmas when employing the same criteria used to define dilemmas in teaching. As hanging chads, the security of electronic voting machines, and hand-by-hand recounting of ballots in close elections illustrate, even the problem of tallying votes can quickly turn to a dilemma of competing values, unattractive choices, and compromise. Even when an election's outcome is solved, further dilemmas may wait ahead.

Responding to most political issues facing the U.S. public, like responding to the teaching dilemmas described earlier, requires acknowledging the value-laden nature of these dilemmas, framing them without blame, and walking a tightrope between competing values. Just as in teaching, instructors should frame questions about democratic dilemmas by asking either explicitly or implicitly what should be done. How should the lines for an election district be drawn—by balancing the party affiliation of potential voters, by creating a district likely to elect a representative from a particular race or ethnic group, or by following natural boundaries of geography and metropolitan settlement? How should a bill on climate change pass—by holding out until enough legislators sign on to a bill with significant change, by compromising and getting as many legislators on board now in the hope that something is better than nothing, or by horse trading on nonclimate issues to broaden support for the bill?

As anyone who watches U.S. House of Representatives floor debates on C-SPAN, listens to talk radio, or reads partisan blogs knows, politicians, commentators, and writers do not always frame the dilemmas behind public issues without blame. Consequently, the airwaves were full of loaded words and phrases such as "rationing medical service," "taking away patient choice," and "government medical plans" during the debate on health care at the beginning of President Obama's administration. Reviving the economy is framed as choice between Wall Street and Main Street. Social issues such as abortion and same-sex marriage provoke even more partisan language, leaving even less room for political compromise.

Balancing competing values is difficult, not only because of the language in politics but because of the passions and perspectives behind the language. When someone believes the future of Earth is at stake, compromise on climate legislation amounts to planetary suicide. By the same token, if someone believes the future of the U.S. economy is at stake, not compromising on climate legislation dooms millions of workers to unemployment or low-paying jobs. Just as with teaching dilemmas, political dilemmas call for satisficing.

Dilemmas of Service-Learning for Learning About Politics and Democracy

Service-learning is a pedagogy that has been used to contextualize and deepen learning about knowledge in the disciplines, promote civic involvement, and more recently encourage political engagement. Service-learning is seen as a way to motivate students, meet community needs, and make the content of college courses relevant to the world beyond campus. Just as often, it is also perceived as a value-neutral, apolitical teaching strategy. Indeed, funding for service-learning through the Corporation for National and Community Service forbids projects that are politically partisan, such as campaigning on behalf of candidates or referenda, lobbying, or organizing rallies.

Even when service-learning is not used to support partisan political activity, however, it is still value laden and political. It is value laden in the sense that students learn moral and ethical lessons whether or not they were intended by their instructors. For example, students serving in a homeless shelter as part of a public policy course on housing might conclude that such work is more valuable than any debate about housing policy, that politicians do not understand the scope of the problem (but that students themselves do based on one volunteer experience), or that some people without shelter are more "deserving" of help than others.

Service-learning is also political, not in the sense that faculty encourage students to vote a certain way or support some points of view over others, but in the sense that faculty and students engaged in service make choices and learn lessons that have a political dimension. When faculty require service from students in a course, decide to partner with some community agencies and not others, and select texts to contextualize public issues and frame reflection on service, they are shaping students' political learning. Even when faculty decide not to use service-learning, they are making a choice that is not without a political element.

Because service-learning, perhaps more than other teaching strategies, is based on value-laden and political assumptions and because it shapes values and political lessons, it is a valuable means of preparing students for political engagement. To do so, however, the value-laden and political dimension of service-learning needs to be an explicit part of instruction rather than something to be avoided, which is an impossibility in any case.

How to make this dimension of service-learning explicit is probably more obvious in some disciplines and academic departments than others. For example, a political science professor offering a politics of education class can make students' service in local schools an opportunity for them to consider the reasons behind and consequences of current K–12 education funding at the federal and state level, debate a local parcel tax initiative to support schools, and critique various ways to measure and reward school effectiveness.

Contextualizing the political dimension of learning from service might seem less obvious in disciplines seen as apolitical, such as engineering, child development, or Spanish language and literature. Many students—and perhaps some faculty—will think that learning about bridge building, preschool curriculum, or the culture of Spanish-speaking countries has no political element. But bridges are designed and constructed because of political appropriations, preschool curriculum is required to meet standards set by policy makers, and countries in Latin America share a political culture that has not been and is not without U.S. influence.

Consequently, service-learning in any discipline can be a vehicle for political learning. Engineering students engaged in service-learning can use their experience to raise questions about current transportation policy, to deepen their understanding of the politics of infrastructure spending, and to understand the role of public participation in local communities affected by new construction. Child development students can connect their service to local debates about community standards for teaching certain subjects, school committee resolutions on opening or closing child development centers, and candidates' stances on Head Start. Language students serving at a local community center in a Spanish-speaking neighborhood can reflect on the effects of legislation limiting services only to U.S. citizens, the relative political power of those being served as individuals and a group, and the potential of community centers for educating others on political participation.

Dilemmas as Essential Aspects of Teaching

Because teaching is an uncertain act full of dilemmas, service-learning is bound to be no different. And service-learning with an expressed goal of preparing students with political knowledge, skills, and dispositions is even more likely to present uncertainty and dilemmas. To gain the most value from service-learning for political engagement, it is important to make the political dimension of service explicit and to exploit, not avoid, the dilemmas that inevitably result. In this way, dilemmas are not an obstacle to implementing service-learning for political engagement; they are a valuable part of the process.

Capitalizing on dilemmas does not mean neglecting to plan or failing to be intentional because dilemmas happen. Rather, it means recognizing that dilemmas are an inevitable part of democratic life, teaching and learning, and service-learning in particular. It means envisioning what dilemmas might occur and deciding which are productive and which might be less productive and minimized if possible. It means developing plans for responding to—not solving—dilemmas with educative potential. And it means being explicit with students about how acknowledging and addressing dilemmas is part of learning generally and part of learning for democratic life.

As instructors think about dilemmas that might develop in service-learning practice, they should consider these types that are common to the pedagogy:

- *Dilemmas about the kind of service.* Should service be situated in organizations providing services to remedy immediate problems from hunger to polluted beaches or in organizations working on longer-term solutions? Should service be situated in nonpartisan organizations or in groups with particular political views, in groups with a technical focus or with a more explicitly value-laden approach such as working toward social justice? Should service provide direct contact with diverse people or lean toward community research of public issues?
- *Dilemmas about discourse on political issues.* Is the classroom floor open to any and all opinions or do boundaries define acceptable discussion? Do faculty reveal their own opinions in discussion, share them last, or pretend to be neutral? Is the purpose of political discourse to convince others or to question one's own ideas? Who decides who speaks—teachers, students, an invisible hand? Why do students speak—because they are loudest, because they have a turn, because they are solicited for an opinion?

- *Dilemmas about making decisions.* How are decisions made in the classroom—by voting, by consensus, by instructor fiat?
- *Dilemmas about course content.* What gets taught in depth, what is mentioned, what is left out? Are disagreement and contention considered natural parts of coming to know in the discipline, or is disciplinary knowledge understood as beyond debate? Is truth in the discipline considered socially constructed or individually discovered? How many sides of any subject matter issue are presented? How are decisions made about which sides are considered legitimate?

With these and other dilemmas, it is helpful to know how others frame and respond to dilemmas. In classrooms where service-learning is geared toward education for practicing democracy, students should learn how a variety of people have framed and responded to dilemmas with political implications. They should learn the most accepted framings as well as those considered unpopular; impractical; or too much, too soon. After all, in addition to addressing current realities, democratic participation requires envisioning beyond the status quo. Looking at historical examples of reframing in politics can help students understand that compromise is not always about splitting the differences in responses but proposing a different dilemma to be addressed in the first place. For example, ending discrimination in schooling has been reframed from separate but equal to integration to closing the achievement gap. As another example, health care has been reframed from a medical issue to a social justice issue to an economic issue.

Students should not only understand how others frame and reframe political issues, they should gain practice in the framing and reframing process themselves. This requires seeing issues from multiple perspectives, envisioning responses beyond what has been tried, and unveiling the varying—and perhaps competing—values inherent in those responses. Dilemmas in the classroom present opportunities for engaging in such practice. Before making a decision or asking students what to do, ask, Is this a problem or a dilemma? How might this be framed? How does a particular framing contribute to understanding how to respond? How might that response lead to other issues later?

As the teaching cases by Lynne Bercaw and Caroline Heldman in Chapters 2 and 3, respectively, illustrate, reflective practice fully includes our instructors' educational actions and decisions as they struggle to make service-learning courses meaningful democratic experiences. If dilemmas are part of classroom and democratic life, then instructors can capitalize on classroom dilemmas by using them to educate students for political participation in democracy. Service-learning, like any pedagogy, raises dilemmas. With its emphasis on reflection, however, service-learning can provide an exceptional way to become more knowledgeable, skilled, and motivated to participate effectively in the political messiness and contention of the real world.

References

Cuban, L. (2001). *How can I fix it? Finding solutions and managing dilemmas.* New York, NY: Teachers College Press.

Dewey, J. (1904). *School and society.* Chicago, IL: University of Chicago Press.

2

BANNING BOOKS TO PROTECT CHILDREN

Clashing Perspectives in Service-Learning

Lynne A. Bercaw

Having implemented service-learning in my children's literature course for 8 years, I was initially not worried about service-learning projects related to political engagement that might be in direct opposition to my values and opinions. Over the years, students in my course have conducted projects that ranged from collecting books to writing books for children. What I failed to see, however, was how the addition of a political engagement component inherently opens service-learning projects to varying values and opinions, when the political dimension of selecting, making available, assigning, and interpreting children's literature becomes explicit.

Course Contexts

I teach a graduate course on children's literature in which I introduced a service-learning for political engagement assignment. I began by engaging students in a discussion of the ways children's literature is political. At the end of the discussion, we had a rich body of ideas (e.g., censorship, power of literacy, publishing, etc.). Informed by these ideas, each student selected a topic and designed a project around it. The broad guideline of the assignment was that each service-learning project should have a political focus in the field of children's literature. Throughout the semester, students submitted their ideas for their projects for my feedback and guidance.

As expected, each project was as different as each student, and some projects were clearer than others about political engagement. One student created an information pamphlet regarding literacy advocacy through service dogs (dogs that "listen" to struggling readers, providing a nonjudgmental audience). Another student wrote letters to various state and federal representatives regarding reading legislation, specifically in relation to the No Child Left Behind Act of 2001. Yet another focused on the political implications of literacy and citizenship by introducing the public library to children from low socioeconomic homes and providing them with library cards.

Several students designed projects on censorship, each student approaching the concept in a different way. For example, one project entailed a letter to the local school board regarding book selection and the danger of book banning in a democratic society. Another student created a pamphlet that highlighted various controversial books that should be included in school libraries and a rationale for each. While each project differed in nature, they all took a similar perspective against censorship except for one—Jim's. His project focused on censoring a book he found offensive.

Democratic Dilemma

To understand Jim and his perspective, it is important to understand the context of his project. The first novel we discussed as a class was *The Giver*, a classic work in children's literature by Lois Lowry (1994/2003). In 1994 *The Giver* received the Newbery Medal, the highest honor awarded for excellence in literature for children. The story is about a society where almost (or "nearly") everything is controlled, from the way one looks to the release, or elimination, of those who in some way do not fit in to the society. Because of references to abortion, genetic selection, euthanasia, and teenage "stirrings," this book is one of the most frequently banned books in the United States (American Library Association, 2007).

In our discussion, Jim was visibly agitated and shared that he was deeply offended by the content of the novel. He expressed his disdain for it and the inappropriateness of the book for children. Other students, mostly librarians and teachers, tried to explain the merits of the book; however, Jim held firm that not only was this book offensive to him as an adult, but it was undeniably inappropriate for children. He had disturbing dreams about it and had to force himself to finish the book—which he did only because it was an assigned reading.

I have had students in the past ask to be excused from reading books such as *Harry Potter* and am sensitive to honoring students' values and beliefs while still trying to challenge them (Bercaw, 2003). With this in mind, I e-mailed the student after class, because *The Giver* was the first of many controversial books we would be reading in class. His response was as follows:

> My concerns about *The Giver* are many. Children should not have to deal with something like the intentional death of an infant—reading this atrocity in a book should not be something my child or any child should have in their minds. That is why I believe the school district should remove it from the classroom.

In the next class session, Jim was even more agitated and described what had happened after the last class. His fifth-grade daughter brought *The Giver* home, having checked the book out from her teacher's classroom library. Jim asked why she chose this book, to which his daughter replied that she saw her dad reading it for a children's literature class and wanted to read it as well. (Most literature and language arts instructors give a mighty cheer that a child wants to emulate an adult's reading choice.) Jim was "horrified" to see the book in his child's hands. The next day, he brought the book to the principal's office and demanded he remove each copy of the book from the school. The principal said he couldn't do that.

Pedagogical Approach

Coincidentally, the topic for the next class session was censorship. I addressed the issue by representing different points of view regarding censorship. Students read different position statements from leading organizations in reading such as the American Library Association (2004), National Council of Teachers of English (2009), and International Reading Association (1985), all of which advocate against forms of censorship. They also read position statements on parents' rights in book selection from organizations such as Focus on the Family (2009) and Family Research Council (2009). Ultimately, I shared the problems with censorship in light of intellectual freedom, which resonates with the professional organizations in advocating against the banning of books.

Jim's experience with his daughter's coming home with the book from her teacher's library and the principal's refusal to remove the book from the school became the springboard for his service-learning/political engagement project—a persuasive letter to the school board to ban *The Giver*.

For the service-learning project I asked the same questions of all students: (a) What service does the project provide? (b) How will the project deepen one's understanding of children's literature? and (c) How is the project political? Jim explained that he was providing a service to children by protecting them from offensive literature, that his understanding of children's literature was deepened through exploring what makes quality literature, and that it was political because he was advocating for children by influencing policy. Further, he stated that he was exercising his voice and his right in the decisions in public schooling.

In addition to the conflicting views between Jim and me, there was also the community Jim was seeking to serve, which I needed to explore and honor. In the spirit of intellectual freedom, individuals have the right to pursue information without restriction. Jim's pursuit led him to block the pursuit of others in his community, yet the community has the right to allow intellectual freedom for its citizens. As a service-learning instructor, I had the responsibility to honor my student and our community partner.

Teaching Dilemma

Jim's stance on censorship was in sharp contrast to mine, which gives a compelling case of two clashing democratic values: freedom of opinion and freedom of information. This dilemma involved my struggle with the competing concerns of allowing Jim to express his opinion with the equally prized concern of intellectual freedom and allowing children access to literature from a variety of perspectives. My first line of framing the problem was that Jim *could not* do his proposed project because it flies in the face of the course goals and of what would be expected of a student in a master's-level reading program.

Reframing the problem was far more challenging as I tried to "invent new ways to interpret" the situation (Cuban, 2001, p. 24). My first action was to step back and assess the purpose of the project and what I hold true as an educator to be the purpose of education. I then could consider Jim's proposal for his project through a new lens and saw several avenues I could pursue with him. I was continually drawn to intellectual freedom and what that meant for me and my students. I was torn between wanting to honor Jim's perspective, and in the spirit of his intellectual and political freedom allowing him to proceed with his project as planned. Yet, I also had to consider those beyond Jim—the teachers and children in his school district.

The question I wrestled with was, How could I honor their intellectual freedoms as well as Jim's? I could simply accept Jim's proposal as is, which would honor his voice and perspective, yet it would be in sharp contrast to the premise of intellectual freedom for the children in his district. Another option was simply to say the project was unacceptable because it was in contradiction to the goals of the course. He would then have to design another project focusing on a different issue. This would solve the problem of challenging intellectual freedom; however, I felt it would also silence Jim's perspective. Another option was to work with Jim to modify his project in a way that would not compromise his position yet also not infringe upon the rights of others in his district. The dilemma with this option was that I would ultimately be leading Jim away from a project and position he was passionate about.

Instructional Strategy: Framing and Reframing

Ultimately, I decided on the last option based on an effort to honor Jim's voice and intellectual freedom and those of whom he was aiming to serve. I therefore guided him away from the project where the service was banning *The Giver*. The compromise was that Jim would write a letter to the school's principal asking him to require teachers to read each book in their classroom libraries. Jim argued that had his daughter's classroom teacher read *The Giver*, she would have known that the book was not appropriate for his daughter and subsequently could have guided her to another book that honored his family's values.

This dilemma provided the opportunity for my students and me to engage in the work of democracy: framing and reframing issues. Rather than presenting students with only two options, freedom of opinion and book banning or censoring opinion and no book banning, we explored other ways to frame the issue, thus allowing for other ways to resolve the dilemma. In the end, after realizing that the teacher had not read *The Giver* before putting it on her sixth-grade classroom's reading shelf, Jim decided that a more appropriate project would be to craft a school policy requiring teachers to read all books before placing them on shelves for students. This honored his concerns as a parent and teacher and honored my values regarding intellectual freedom and access to literature.

This resolution matched intellectual freedom with the responsibility to help young people make appropriate choices for their reading. In addition to being grounded in best practices of organizations concerned about children's literature, such as the American Library Association, the National Council of Teachers of English, and the International Reading Association, the resolution also respected the student's agency. In the end, students in this children's literature course realized that democracy is not necessarily about winning over others to one's point of view but framing political issues so all parties feel vested in the eventual outcome.

In Jim's final project, however—a letter to the principal requesting all teachers read the books in their classroom libraries—I questioned whether Jim *really* had the ownership of his project that he said he did. He started his letter with the statement that he was writing this letter because he "needed the course credit." The message I took from this was that he *had not* bought into the reframing of the problem. He still believed that banning *The Giver* was really what needed to be done to protect children.

Reflection and Insights

In thinking about implementing this project in my future children's literature courses, several aspects of this experience inform my planning. My value of bringing students' voices to the projects is inherent by the design of the service-learning project—students choose the political issue they want to pursue as an academic inquiry and as a service to the community. This open-ended approach, however, requires the instructor to be more open to the types of projects students conduct and sensitive to reframing them in ways so students consider multiple perspectives. Just as literature can challenge readers to grapple with multiple perspectives, service with a focus on political engagement requires the same grappling to frame democratic dilemmas. The sphere of openness is where deep, critical probing poses the dilemmas that ultimately lead to a sharper understanding of one's value's, of one's place in the community, and of one's role as a civic participant in the community.

The implication from the experience with Jim demonstrates that when students and instructors can approach a dilemma with framing and reframing in mind, all participants' perspectives have the potential to be honored. As Jim demonstrated in the very end, however, there is also the risk that despite all the conversation and discussion, the student acquiesces because of the power structure and because of an ultimate goal of passing the course. Despite communicating with him that his grade would not be affected by the nature of the project, his fear of the grading power I held over him proved more influential as he completed his final project. The implication of this is that a foundation of trust of my genuine expectations is communicated and honored. In other words, it is my responsibility to make my expectations and all agendas transparent.

References

American Library Association. (2004). *The freedom to read statement.* Retrieved from http://www.ala.org/ala/aboutala/offices/oif/statementspols/ftrstatement/freedom readstatement.cfm

American Library Association. (2007). *Lois Lowry honored for lifetime contribution to young adult readers with Edwards Award.* Retrieved from http://www.ala.org/ala/newspresscenter/news/pressreleases2007/january2007/edwards07.cfm

Bercaw, L. (2003). Small victories: Reflections on teaching *Harry Potter* to resistant prospective teachers. *Journal of Children's Literature, 29*(1), 32–35.

Cuban, L. (2001). *How can I fix it? Finding solutions and managing dilemmas.* New York, NY: Teachers College Press.

Family Research Council. (2009). *Marriage & family.* Retrieved from http://www.frc.org/marriage-family#rights

Focus on the Family. (2009). *Book reviews for parents.* Retrieved 10 June 2009 from http://www.focusonthefamily.com/parenting/protecting_your_family/book_reviews_for_parents.aspx

International Reading Association. (1985). *International Reading Association censorship statement.* Retrieved from http://psba.org/districts_policies/P/484/POLPLEA 109_1AppG.pdf

Lowry, L. (2003). *The giver.* New York, NY: Houghton Mifflin.

National Council of Teachers of English. (1981/2009). *Guideline on the students' right to read.* Retrieved from http://www.ncte.org/positions/statements/righttoread guideline

3

SOLIDARITY, NOT CHARITY

Issues of Privilege in Service-Learning

Caroline Heldman

C ommunity-based learning (CBL) placements that involve college students working with disadvantaged populations may involve students' enacting their privilege in ignorant and insensitive ways. This teaching vignette explores issues that arise with student privilege in political CBL work, and pedagogical approaches that address these issues through a case study of student work in New Orleans.

Course Overview

Over 200 liberal arts students from California have worked on the post-Katrina Gulf Coast through the course Disaster Politics: New Orleans in the Wake of Hurricane Katrina. This class combines academic work and political activism with the primary goal of enabling students to recognize the causes and consequences of the delayed response to Hurricane Katrina. The course emphasizes the human-made aspects of the disaster with particular emphasis on national, state, and local government responses. Emphasis is also placed on the atrocities surrounding the storm: the New Orleans Mississippi River bridge incident where local law enforcement officials from the city of Gretna on the West Bank stopped evacuees at the Orleans/Jefferson Parish border with dogs and gunfire (Throgmorton, 2008); the Danziger Bridge incident where police officers opened fire on six locals crossing the bridge to get to a supermarket, killing two residents (Foster, 2010); the mass closure of public housing units that were only minimally damaged (Palast, 2007); and roving gangs of White vigilantes in Algiers Point who killed at least 11 Black residents (Thompson, 2008). Students also learn about political decisions that were made after the storm that worked against equitable rebuilding in the region, including delayed revitalization of poor neighborhoods, the suspension of Affirmative Action requirements for contractors, temporary suspension of the prevailing wages in the region, and what Naomi Klein (2008) has termed *disaster capitalism*—the granting of no-bid contracts during times of crisis.

Working in New Orleans

After reading and writing about the events of Hurricane Katrina, students live and work for three weeks in the Lower Ninth Ward with Common Ground Relief, a grassroots organization started by local residents shortly after Katrina hit. Work activities include mucking (removing the waterlogged contents of homes), gutting (interior demolition of houses) and rebuilding homes, removing debris and trash from neighborhoods, remediating mold, planting trees in the wetlands, tutoring children, and working in a women's shelter.

Students are also encouraged to get involved in local political actions on their own time, and most do. Students have organized protests and sit-ins and attended community organizing workshops, antiracism working groups, and talks by local activists. During different class trips, students protested against the demolition of public housing units, met families who are not eligible for Road Home money even though they lost everything in the storm, and mowed the now empty lots of land belonging to residents who do not have the means to return home and are in danger of losing their property to the government. Some students have witnessed police brutality against local Black residents, watched a stream of cars driving by a homeless man who was hit by a car on a busy road, and served hot food to individuals living in a homeless encampment. Many students have been harassed by police and National Guard officers about their presence in Black neighborhoods. Student experiences vary in terms of the type of work performed, encounters with local residents, and observations of injustice, but students universally leave the region with broken hearts and confusion about their place in the world. They also leave with elevated political efficacy and a desire to be more active in politics and social justice work back home.

Politically engaged CBL experiences have quite positive learning outcomes for students, but they run the risk of offending community members through insensitive student actions, as well as furthering problematic race and socioeconomic hierarchies through "charity" work.

Issues of Privilege

One of the downsides of CBL work is student privilege that manifests itself in insensitive and ignorant ways. Privilege is defined as a set of advantages enjoyed by one group that are not commonly experienced by another group. In the case of New Orleans, many students unwittingly brought White privilege and class privilege to the CBL experience. Some instances involved insensitive encounters with residents directly, while others involved a general disrespect for the community.

Overall, students were respectful in their direct encounters with local residents, but this was not always the case. Some students showed disrespect for local speakers as compared to other guest speakers by not paying attention, falling asleep, or walking out during their talks. One student refused food offered by a local resident on her work site, proclaiming that it was "smelly." I also received several complaints from crew leaders (returning students from a previous course) regarding issues while working in residents' homes. With residents present, students would joke around with their furniture and belongings and make callous comments about the small size of the homes, suggesting that they weren't worth saving. Another frequent complaint was students' heavy handling of furniture—treating the mucking process like an extreme sport by throwing furniture around and smashing items in the process, sometimes with a grieving resident sitting on the front porch.

Disrespect of the community as opposed to specific residents was more common. Students would frequently walk through neighborhoods in large noisy groups and snap pictures of residents and their homes without their permission. During one of our trips to the Gulf Coast, a local resident was so offended by such behaviors (from another college group) that he pretended to hold them up at gunpoint to teach them a lesson about treating his neighborhood like a zoo. Students also frequently treated damaged homes as public property, sitting on their porches or urinating in backyards. Some of the more egregious acts of insensitivity toward the community included students' arriving at the volunteer site in a limousine that wound its way through the devastated Ninth Ward; students sunbathing on the concrete slabs of homes that had been washed away in the storm; and a student holding her nose while serving hot meals to local residents while wearing designer clothes (midriff bared), high heels, and a Louis Vuitton purse slung over her shoulder.

These insensitive actions of privilege go hand in hand with the paradigm of performing *charity* work instead of *solidarity* work. With charity work, volunteers conceive of themselves as being above the person or group they are assisting. They see their assistance as one-sided instead of recognizing the benefits they receive in the exchange (e.g., feeling good about themselves, learning from the people they are assisting, living a more meaningful life). Charity workers believe their volunteer work makes them "good people," and they expect recognition for it. In my experience, the vast majority of students go to New Orleans because this is sexy volunteer work for which they will receive many pats on the back when they return, as opposed to more mundane local volunteer work.

The alternative paradigm is solidarity work where volunteers (a) see themselves as equal to the people they are assisting, (b) are able to see how privilege shapes their place in the social/economic hierarchy, (c) see a part of themselves in the person they are working with, (d) recognize they are working for the betterment of both parties, and (e) understand they are working for their own liberation from systems of supremacy that they unconsciously uphold through their everyday actions. With a solidarity approach, the focus of the work shifts from the volunteer to a long-term partnership in which volunteers provide concrete support to an oppressed group so they can more easily use their own power to change the condition of their lives (McClure, 2006).

Pedagogical Strategies

My initial response to the insensitive actions of privilege described here was to get angry at the offending students. I had assumed a certain level of sensitivity on their part considering they were giving up their winter break to live and work in a devastated region. I failed to recognize the various possible motivations for going to New Orleans: recognition for their good deeds upon their return, Bourbon Street and ready access to alcohol, and a trip away from Los Angeles on the college's dime, to name a few. My pedagogical response was to revamp the course to "meet the students where they are" without providing too large a space for ignorance.

First, I added readings that directly addressed issues of privilege. The question of what it means to engage in solidarity versus charity work is now one of the defining aspects of the curriculum. Students are encouraged to examine what they know about poverty work in their own hometowns, why they chose to volunteer in New Orleans versus engaging in poverty work at home, how they benefit from volunteering in the Louisiana region, the ethics of going to a region when many residents cannot afford to return home, how the money spent on their trip might be better spent helping residents in other ways, the power dynamics inherent in privileged mostly White students coming to help poor mostly Black residents, how student privilege colors engagement with the community, and why some local residents are not happy about the presence of student volunteers.

Second, I incorporated questions of privilege into our evening meetings while in New Orleans. A safe space was created where students could report on and admit to actions of privilege during professor- and peer-guided discussions. If no examples were available for analysis, I would provide examples from past student trips as well as my own enactments of privilege. This proved to be an invaluable method for revealing the complicated ways White privilege and class privilege function in everyday life.

Students were also directed to keep a journal about their privilege through several prompts: In what ways are you privileged, and what benefits do you receive from this privilege? How did you enact your race/class/gender privilege today? Is it possible to use privilege to help those who are less privileged without furthering this power imbalance? Many students reported epiphanies in their journals:

> We, as "white," define ourselves as superior and the norm, contrary to "Black," which conjures up notions of a less civilized nature. . . . I can say confidently that I do not believe I would be here if I were not "white" and middle-class. Because of my combined racial and socioeconomic status, I have been put in a position to take advantage of many opportunities afforded to me, and one is I can afford this trip.
>
> I am privileged in that I can count on having a home and a family to go back to. Standing on a cement driveway and no home behind it was the

first time I felt uncontrollably sad. This family had no home to come back to.

Last, I added a new module to the training of crew leaders to empower them to spot and address acts of insensitivity on the work site. Crew leaders are now encouraged to step in when they witness acts of sexism, homophobia, racism, and classism and are empowered to lead evening discussions about these experiences as teachable moments. This strategy has been quite effective as students seem more open to hear criticism from their peers as opposed to their professor. In one case, a student downloaded an article for the class to read about the link between sexism and homophobia to address the sexual harassment and homophobia he observed at his work site. The discussion linked the White supremacy and class supremacy systems to other interlocking systems of oppression (e.g., gender, sexuality) in such a way that students could relate it to their own experiences.

Conclusion

CBL experiences may involve students' enacting their social and economic privilege in insensitive ways, but these actions and their underlying attitudinal causes can be effectively addressed through a curriculum that continually converts ignorant acts into teachable moments, and compels students to critically unpack their privilege. These issues are related to the larger problem that some CBL courses create inherently exploitative situations where students benefit more from the life-changing experience than the community benefits from their unskilled labor. The simple fact that it costs about $25,000 to bring 50 students to New Orleans for a few weeks to perform grunt work that is probably taking jobs away from local residents is clear evidence of an exploitative relationship. Perhaps this calls for a paradigm shift in how we conceive of student-community partnerships—one that recognizes that students often get more out of their experience than they can possibly give, as well as professors who capitalize on these experiences for publication.

References

Foster, M. (2010, June 4). *Ex-cop pleads guilty in Katrina bridge shooting*. Associated Press. http://abcnews.go.com/US/wireStory?id=10827271

Klein, N. (2008). *The shock doctrine: The rise of disaster capitalism*. New York, NY: Picador.

McClure, M. (2006). *Solidarity not charity: Racism in Katrina relief work*. Retrieved from http://www.cwsworkshop.org/katrinareader/node/461

Palast, G. (2007). *Five years and still drowning: The New Orleans CNN would never show you*. Retrieved from http://www.gregpalast.com/

Thompson, A. C. (2008, December 17). Katrina's hidden race war. *The Nation, 288*(1), 11–18.

Throgmorton, J. (2008). The bridge to Gretna: Three faces of a case. *Planning Theory & Practice, 9*(2), 187–208.

PART TWO

DESIGNING SERVICE-LEARNING COURSES FOR DEMOCRATIC OUTCOMES

4

PEDAGOGICAL AND EPISTEMOLOGICAL APPROACHES TO SERVICE-LEARNING

Connecting Academic Content to Community Service

Christine M. Cress

"The experience confirmed my view that homeless people are lazy, crazy, or both."

"If parents just got involved with their kid's education, we wouldn't have to be here tutoring them."

"You would think Native people would care more about not trashing their own land."

Dilemmas of Service-Learning Course Design

Even those instructors who carefully craft their service-learning courses to make connections between academic content, community challenges, and democratic outcomes have received disappointingly stereotypic reactions from students via class comments and journal reflections. As Lynne Bercaw and Caroline Heldman illustrated in the two previous chapters, students may also choose to apply their new knowledge and skills in ways counter to course objectives. In fact, faculty with the best of curricular goals in mind report that their efforts have at times unintentionally reinforced narrow conceptions of individuals and organizations especially if students maintain their perceptions of the service as charity rather than as reciprocal learning opportunities for examining underlying antecedents of community issues (Cress, Kerrigan, & Reitenauer, 2003).

To be perfectly honest, designing and teaching a service-learning course is not an easy task. As David Donahue pointed out in Chapter 1, faculty must answer for themselves critical questions concerning the type of service involvement, discourse about service-learning, course content, and authority roles for students and faculty in decision making. What community agency will make the best learning site? How can the course model and facilitate democratic skills and knowledge that are solidly embedded within academic traditions? What should students read? What should they research? And what should they do to best enhance their own abilities and the potential assets of their communities?

Other challenges and dilemmas that often face faculty include students' resistance to the idea of serving when they are paying tuition to receive knowledge; students' lack of responsibility, reliability, and dependability—clients and community agencies waste time, money, and resources if students don't show up on time (or at all) or don't complete projects; community agency fluctuation in funding and personnel that may affect site access and student support; community partner expectations that do not align with academic goals; faculty uncertainty about when to guide students' experiences and when direct intervention is necessary; and department or administrative doubt that service-learning is a legitimate pedagogical strategy. Indeed, you may be asking yourself right now, if I undertake a service-learning course will this help or hurt me in the tenure and promotion process?

While not every issue can be addressed through thoughtful course design, ensuring effective learning processes and outcomes is to a large extent requisite upon a strong syllabus. Moreover, design and revision of a service-learning course should be viewed as an extension of the *Scholarship of Teaching* and the *Scholarship of Engagement* described by Boyer (1990) as an essential purpose of professorial roles and responsibilities in connecting academe with the functions of democratic communities. As such, service-learning is proven as an effective pedagogy for student learning of academic content, knowledge, and skills (Astin, Vogelgesang, et al., 2006; Cress, Yamashita, Duarte, & Burns, 2010; Prentice & Robinson, 2010) and a source for research and scholarship on community issues, community impact, and community improvement (Hollander & Burack, 2009; Vogelgesang, Denson, & Jayakumar, 2010).

The following are pedagogical strategies for constructing service-learning courses. These are not intended to be prescriptive but rather are drawn from approaches that have well served the contributors to this book. Certainly instructors should frame their courses from their own expertise and organizational context. It is hoped the ideas below can add to the reader's knowledge repertoire for realizing successful service-learning.

Strategy 1: Course Descriptions

To start, service-learning must be integrated and not just added to existing courses. Faculty who simply tack on service hours and requirements usually find themselves frustrated because there are fewer hours to spend on content. Concurrently, students usually express anxiety that course obligations have increased without direct relevance to their academic major.

Often, official course descriptions cannot be revised in college catalogs without a myriad of bureaucratic approval processes taking enormous amounts of time. However, that should not preclude instructors from including the service-learning component in their syllabus course descriptions.

Tom Trice at California Polytechnic State University, San Luis Obispo, accomplishes this through a bilevel description of his history course, European Thought and Culture: 1750–Present. The first level is the department course description, and the second level describes how service-learning deepens understanding of the academic content.

- This course explores the relationship between the individual, society, and government in the context of major intellectual, cultural, and social forces that shaped European life from the mid-eighteenth century to the present.
- Through community-based learning, this course encourages you to consider the extent to which such forces have affected, or may yet influence, the ways in which we experience and understand our own roles in an increasingly complex, global society. This dual focus permits us to examine what remains a highly contentious issue in modern Europe and much of the world: the proper relationship between

theory and praxis. (T. R. Trice, personal communication, January 11, 2008)

By connecting issues in history with contemporary challenges through community involvement, Trice has created a parsimonious synergy between content and community for academic learning. Similarly, Christopher Brooks (below and see Chapter 17 for more course information) offers his computer science students a translation of the formal course description and actual service-learning engagement:

- Course description: Computer and network security measures, encryption protocols. Ethical theory and applications in computing.
- Translation: This course is about the ways computers and information technology affect our lives and society. It's about the moral and ethical choices we are faced with as producers and consumers of computing technology. It's also about the political dimensions of information technology and the ways these areas influence each other.
- What's the class like? Monday and Wednesday are class days, and Friday is on site where you will be performing service-learning with a community partner.
- What's this service thing? You will be working with a community agency that provides computer access, training, and support to local communities. The experience will allow you to apply your technology knowledge and skills in directly helping others and also give you firsthand insights into the ways technology can affect the lives of the disenfranchised.

Brooks anticipates his students may not only be confused by but skeptical of service-learning and addresses this in the first page of his syllabus. Of course, as Dari Sylvester states in Chapter 5, just putting the academic purposes of service-learning in writing will not necessarily deter vocal student objections. It is hoped instructors can use negative queries and comments as teachable moments in the classroom. Still, directly connecting the course to the community from the outset will help students understand the learning parameters of the class.

Strategy 2: Learning Objectives

Students will also have a better understanding of the nature of the course through well-structured learning outcomes and objectives. Normally, learning objectives are written as end products of the course experience: As a result of the class, what will students know and be able to do? Often, service-learning objectives go a step further in defining how the experience might shift students' feelings, attitudes, and motivations.

Attending to the affective development of students has been long seen as crucial to the capacity building of our businesses, government, and neighborhoods. Bowen (1977) states that hope for our nation lies in our investment in learning of the whole person through the cultivation of the intellect, the honing of practical competence, and the development of affective dispositions. Indeed, research has shown that critical thinking and judgment are dependent upon the effective interplay of cognitive and affective dimensions (Goleman, 1995).

Moreover, researchers (Kegan, 2000; Mezirow, 1991) and other educators (Hurtado, 2010; Keeling, 2004) agree that truly effective education is one that transforms students' perceptions of the world into new forms of conscious decision making and action. For example, students will better understand critical academic concepts such as those in the discipline of economics:

- Understand the economic challenges of allocating limited resources among competing uses in a global economy and across different market structures.

In addition to understanding the economic concepts, students will be able to better apply their new academic skills:

- Effectively access, analyze, and interpret economic data and how these variables affect public policy.

Finally, students will become aware of future opportunities as economic professionals to influence the distribution of resources in their communities and be motivated to help create positive community change:

- Understand how their careers can impact the larger world and indicate interest in future community involvement and leadership.

Can students accomplish these types of academic, skill, and attitudinal outcomes without engaging in service-learning? Absolutely, but reading and researching about homelessness is incomparably different from interacting with a homeless individual, especially if that person is a child.

Most faculty tend to write learning objectives based on their own course experiences as a student or they borrow ideas from colleagues. However, one especially useful source is known as Bloom's Taxonomy. Bloom, Englehart, Furst, Hill, and Krathwohl (1956) developed a list of verbs that progress from the cognitively simply to the cognitively complex.

At the knowledge level (first level), learning objectives are measurable and demonstrable using verbs such as list, name, label, record. Obviously, it is then quite easy to reword these learning objectives for test and assessment purposes. For instance, identify the key economic factors leading to homelessness.

Bloom's Taxonomy then advances to comprehension, application, and analysis. The final two levels are synthesis and evaluation, which include recommendations for action. (For a complete description of Bloom's taxonomy see http://www.edpsycinteractive.org/topics/cogsys/bloom.html)

Examples of general service-learning objectives that could be modified, adapted, and specified to particular courses include the following:

- Identify and describe the needs of the community population (knowledge).
- Explain the role of the community organization in addressing needs (comprehension).
- Model professional learning behavior to youth/clients (application).
- Analyze economic, political, and social factors contributing to the challenges (analysis/synthesis).
- Recommend leverage points for creating systemic change on the organizational and community levels (evaluation).

Finally, three other sources for learning objective ideas are the academic discipline especially if there are attendant lists of professional knowledge and skills, the community partner who may have specialized expertise applicable to the course, and the students themselves.

Directly engaging students in developing their own individual as well as overall course learning outcomes can help maximize student interest in and involvement with service-learning. This strategy can also help sustain momentum, as Katja Guenther writes in Chapter 6, if students become disheartened and frustrated by the immensity of community challenges. Revisiting and reformulating learning objectives as a class process in the middle of the academic term can assist students with recognizing gains (even small ones) and achieve more realistic outcomes given class and community contextual constraints.

Strategy 3: Class Activities

Ideally, learning objectives drive class activities. There should be a clear and explicit relationship between what the syllabus (and teacher) indicates that students are supposed to learn and what they read, research, write, discuss, create, present, perform, and do. Nowhere is this more evident than if the service-learning activities are merely additive rather than integrative; students may balk and even drop the course if they don't understand the purpose and process of service-learning.

Service-learning site. The logistics of initiating a community partnership can be daunting. Take advantage of campus centers or offices that specialize in community outreach for volunteer, internship, and/or service opportunities. Personnel should also be able to guide you in any legal or contractual requirements. For example, some food-related community agencies require students to be tested for hepatitis. Students may also need to sign client confidentiality agreements.

Faculty should contact potential community partners in advance of the academic term to mutually determine goals, roles, and responsibilities, although some faculty at Portland State University who teach senior capstone courses require students to identify and form the college-community partnerships. Certainly, having students initiate the partnership can add to the learning dimension of the course. However, most service-learning instructors find that efficiency and effectiveness are increased when long-term reciprocal partnerships are formed (see Part Three for more collaboration ideas).

Depending on the type of service-learning experience (such as direct client support in after-school tutoring or project-based service in developing a community marketing plan for a nonprofit organization) instructors may want to stipulate on the syllabus the required number of service hours or task expectations. Alternatively, they can be formulated as part of the course process—often faculty invite community partners to give guest presentations before students begin their service. It is critical that students have a clear understanding of how to best apply their time, knowledge, and skills.

Course content. Sorting and settling on the correct breadth and depth of readings and research are quandaries for any instructor of any course. Because the service component will take time, the same amount of content cannot be maintained if a regular course is converted to a service-learning course. Moreover, it is likely that students will need information and material on understanding the social, political, economic, ethnic, and cultural contexts of the community partner and the community populations. Linking learning objectives directly with the service tasks and academic content will deepen understanding and the application of knowledge and skills even if faculty must forgo some of the items on their traditional reading list.

One approach for ensuring content and community connections is to use a matrix or spreadsheet. Descending rows on the left side can represent each week of the term. Columns across the top from left to right might represent learning objectives, content themes or topics, course readings, class activities, service activities, and assignments due, to name a few. Thus, at a quick glance, instructors, students, and even community partners can place themselves in the learning community processes.

Assignments. Should service be assessed with a letter grade or pass/fail? Should reflective journals receive a letter grade or pass/fail? Should students receive individual grades or a group grade for collaborative final presentations? Is it possible to give multiple-choice tests in a service-learning course? Or must students simply take essay exams or write final papers?

The answer is yes. Yes, whatever kind of assignments or assessment processes and rubrics (e.g., grading on a curve, gold stars and happy-faces) that faculty believe best facilitate learning and integration can be used. Just as in regular courses, service-learning instructors use a wide spectrum of grading and assignment approaches based upon disciplinary traditions and individual teaching and learning philosophies. Determining which methods most effectively lead toward democratic skill and knowledge development may be an iterative process (see also Chapter 21, on assessment).

Frequently, students are required to keep, share, and turn in reflective journals describing their observations, activities, and insights about their service-learning. Faculty are encouraged to read these periodically throughout the academic term rather than only collecting them during finals week. Otherwise, instructors become aware too late of serious student and community issues, including ethical and legal violations that should have been addressed midterm. In addition, students may need specific guidance on how to reflect critically on their experience. Rather than open-ended journals, many faculty give students progressively more complex questions to support and challenge students' broadening knowledge and experience base (for more on this see Cress, Collier, Reitenauer, & Associates, 2005).

Finally, other classroom teaching and learning activities can help students make connections as well. In Chapter 6 Katja Guenther describes a collage project of dominant images of low-income populations and how she uses course readings to deconstruct these stereotypic concepts. Similarly, Stephanie Stokamer in Chapter 7 describes how her class uses everyday information tools accessible to the majority of the population—newspapers, films, the Internet—to examine social injustices and identify service-learning opportunities for empowerment and community change. However, Stokamer comes to realize that she must attend to students' emotive responses (feelings) to this new knowledge if they are to actually acquire new civic skills. Intellectual paralysis hits Stokamer's students when they become overwhelmed by the scope and complexity of social inequities. A short but informative lecture on these complementary but sometimes competing epistemological processes serves as cognitive and affective salve for students' mental afflictions in helping them make the transition from privileged guilt to informed empowerment.

Strategy 4: Course Processes to Support Differing Epistemologies

To clarify, the term *pedagogy* in this chapter is used synonymously to represent instructional strategies and methods—the external processes of what (content) and how (lecture, tests, service) we teach. The term *epistemology* is used to represent how we learn—the internal processes of coming to know and understand.

Educational psychology, in particular, has an extensive research base on the mental and biological brain functions involved in learning. Developmental psychologists (Knefelkamp, 2003; Perry, 1981) and other educational researchers (Baxter Magolda, 1992; Belenky, Clinchy, Goldberger, & Tarule, 1986; Gardner, 1993; Gilligan, 1982; Kegan, 2000; King and Kitchener, 1994; Mezirow, 1991) have tried to identify learning activities most likely to advance student awareness and consciously informed decision making and action. Probably best known in a wide variety of academic disciplines is Kolb's (1984) work on the epistemological learning cycle.

Kolb's learning style cycle has four primary cognitive process dimensions along which each individual has a favored preference. Debate exists regarding whether these learning style preferences are innate—biological or sociological—or learned patterns of response. Regardless, Kolb asserts that the most fully integrative learning honors (and responds to) individual preferences while offering experiences of learning that are less familiar and less comfortable. Kolb contends that learners must engage with knowledge, information, and experiences that involve opportunities for *reflective observation* (watching, judging), *abstract conceptualization* (thinking, rationalizing), *active experimentation* (doing, behaving), and *concrete experiencing* (sensory, feelings).

Traditional learning courses most readily agree with learners who have epistemological preferences for reflective observation—to listen and watch a lecture—and abstract conceptualization—to read or write a paper or develop a theoretical model. In contrast, service-learning courses most readily agree with learners who favor active experimentation—interacting with new people and products—and concrete experiencing—those who prefer accomplishing practical results that have real impacts on people's lives. Rather than being at odds with one another, traditional courses have room for more active forms of learning and problem solving. In turn, service-learning courses should maintain proven academic traditions of writing, research, and reflection.

In conclusion, faculty who are developing or revising service-learning courses and syllabi can use Kolb's four primary epistemological categories to frame course descriptions, learning objectives, service-site expectations, reflective journal responses, and other class assignments and activities. Indeed, sometimes it is simply a matter of asking during a class discussion, "How did you feel about that community interaction?" in addition to "What do you think about that community interaction?" Recognizing these paradigmatic differences can be an exponential learning experience for students and faculty alike. These subtle but significant nuances in perspective can also shed new light on why class and community dilemmas occur and how they might be reconciled. Thus, an instructor can hope to read a student journal entry like the illustration below:

> "I realize now that while there are individual factors that lead to homelessness, there are multiple economic and societal factors that contribute—not the least of which are policy decisions made by government leaders. We must work with the city council to provide them good data and achievable strategies."

Intentional course design, thoughtful class facilitation, and student reflection on course content theory and community experiences help transform students' views of themselves and their communities. Furthermore, as students gain new academic insights into community issues their efficacy increases for applying their knowledge and skills for positive community change.

References

Astin, A. W., Vogelgesang, L. J., et al. (2006). *Understanding the effects of service-learning: A study of students and faculty.* Los Angeles, CA: Higher Education Research Institute, University of California, Los Angeles.

Baxter Magolda, M. (1992). *Knowing and reasoning in college: Gender-related patterns in students' intellectual development.* San Francisco, CA: Jossey-Bass.

Belenky, M. F., Clinchy, B. M., Goldberger, N. R., & Tarule, J. M. (1986). *Women's ways of knowing: The development of self, voice, and mind.* New York, NY: Basic Books.

Bloom, B. S., Englehart, M. D., Furst, E. J., Hill, W. H., & Krathwohl, D. R. (1956). *Taxonomy of educational objectives. Handbook 1: Domain.* New York, NY: Longmans, Green.

Bowen, H. R. (1977). *Investment in learning: The individual and social value of American higher education.* San Francisco, CA: Jossey-Bass.

Boyer, E. L. (1990). *Scholarship reconsidered: Priorities of the professoriate.* San Francisco, CA: Jossey-Bass.

Cress, C. M., Collier, P. J., Reitenauer, V. L., & Associates. (2005). *Learning through serving: A student guidebook for service-learning across the disciplines.* Sterling, VA: Stylus.

Cress, C. M., Kerrigan, S., & Reitenauer, V. (2003). Making community-based learning meaningful: Faculty efforts to increase student civic engagement skills. *Transformations: The Journal of Inclusive Scholarship and Pedagogy, 14*(2), 87–100.

Cress, C. M., Yamashita, M., Duarte, R., & Burns, H. (2010). A transnational comparison of service-learning as a tool for leadership development. *International Journal of Organizational Analysis, 18*(2), 228–244.

Gardner, H. (1993). *Multiple intelligences: The theory in practice.* New York, NY: Basic.

Gilligan, C. (1982). *In a different voice: Psychological theory and women's development.* Cambridge, MA: Harvard University Press.

Goleman, D. (1995). *Emotional intelligence.* New York, NY: Bantam Books.

Hollander, E., & Burack, C. (2009). *How young people develop long-lasting habits of civic engagement: A conversation on building a research agenda.* Retrieved from http://www.compact.org/wp-content/uploads/2009/05/spencerconversationresearch agenda1.pdf

Hurtado, S. (2010). *Diversity and civic-minded practice: Faculty and student perspectives.* Burlington, VT: New England Regional Campus Compact.

Keeling, R. (Ed.). (2004). *Learning reconsidered: A campus-wide focus on the student experience.* Washington, DC: ACPA/NASPA.

Kegan, R. (2000). What "form" transforms? A constructive-developmental approach to learning. In J. Mezirow & Associates (Eds.), *Learning as transformation* (pp. 35–70). San Francisco, CA: Jossey-Bass.

King, P. M., & Kitchener, K. S. (1994). *Developing reflective judgment: Understanding and promoting intellectual growth and critical thinking in adolescents and adults.* San Francisco, CA: Jossey-Bass.

Knefelkamp, L. L. (2003). The influence of a classic. *Liberal Education, 89*(3), 10–15.

Kolb, D. A. (1984). *Experiential learning: Experience as the source of learning and development.* Englewood Cliffs, NJ: Prentice-Hall.

Mezirow, J. (1991). *Transformative dimensions of adult learning.* San Francisco, CA: Jossey-Bass.

Perry, W. G., Jr. (1981). Cognitive and ethical growth: The making of meaning. In A. W. Chickering (Ed.), *The modern American college* (pp. 76–116). San Francisco, CA: Jossey-Bass.

Prentice, M., & Robinson, G. (2010). *Improving student learning outcomes with service learning.* Washington, DC: American Association of Community Colleges.

Vogelgesang, L. J., Denson, N., & Jayakumar, U. M. (2010). What determines faculty engaged scholarship? *The Review of Higher Education, 33*(4), 437–472.

5

STUDENT OBJECTION TO SERVICE-LEARNING

A Teachable Moment About Political and Community Engagement

Dari E. Sylvester

O n the first day of class I stood before a group of eager college students explaining how this semester would likely be different from any other. This semester I would require 7–10 hours working with a community partner aiding underserved populations and writing and reflecting extensively on their experiences in addition to required readings and lectures. Certain students seemed excited about the opportunity to try something new, and many of those students had already done some form of service-learning in a previous class. However, many others expressed reservations about the service component. Much of the resistance took the form of, "I don't have extra time to devote outside of class" or "How will I get there if I do not have a car?" Perhaps the most direct objection came from a student I'll call Ann.

Student Skepticism and Resistance

Ann was noticeably uncomfortable with the idea of participating in service-learning. She raised her hand and asked, "So, why do we have to do this?" after my enumeration of the many benefits of service-learning from improved learning and writing skills to improved problem-solving skills. I realized that her question wasn't really about why it was required; instead, it seemed like the deeper question was, "How is this really relevant to me?"

I asked a follow-up question to confirm my suspicions. "How do you think the service-learning might affect or improve your learning?" Ann bristled in response: "I dunno. We'll go in, help some poor people, spend a lot of time. Nothing will change, though. They'll still be poor people and I'll just have less time to do homework."

Her skepticism struck the political scientist chord in me. Ann's statements illustrated the same sense of helplessness conveyed by those who choose to opt out of political activity. I realized that other forms of student resistance perhaps more polite or socially acceptable such as, "I am busy and don't have a lot of time for voting," might well be covers for the same underlying sense of frustration with politics and community needs. It became clear that I had to address this resistance head-on.

Instructional Approach

I decided the best way to deflect some of the pressure from Ann and to capitalize on students who had already bought into the idea would be to pose the question to the class. I said, "I'm sure Ann is not the only student who feels this way. Who else shares concerns about the way the service-learning component will affect their schedules and their learning?"

Several hands were raised. I asked who had participated in service-learning before. Three students raised their hand and I directed the following question to them: "What did the service-learning experience teach you that you could not have learned from a book or class lecture?" A couple of students described how they had initially been very reluctant about service-learning because of a fear of homeless populations or because of a fear of the unknown community service element. They said that working with these populations taught them how much the underserved have in common with "regular people" but who had "just had a bad break in life. They were otherwise just like [them]."

Next, I asked students to think of reasons why people don't engage in political activities like voting, writing to a member of Congress, or campaigning for a preferred candidate. Students gave the following reasons: lack of time, lack of interest, lack of skills. However, when I asked students if another possibility was that many people are unsure that the work they put into something will have any real effect—that is, they have a strong suspicion that one vote or that one letter will not have an impact on the political outcome—students nodded in agreement.

I brought the discussion back to service-learning and asked, "Will serving food at a soup kitchen solve the hunger problem? Will handing out blankets to the homeless reduce the number of people without shelter?" Students said no. And Ann chimed in, "Exactly. So why bother?" At this point, I engaged the class to address Ann's opinion. Michael tentatively volunteered, "Well, maybe like writing that letter—there's just some good in having done it. It's a good in itself." I prodded, "Well, why?" He replied, "If you can see what it's like to live that way, maybe you can become better equipped to work in ways that actually do make a difference." Amy added, "And besides, if everyone quit helping because it wouldn't make a difference, then the problems would probably even grow bigger."

Not unlike service-learning, political activity is typically performed by less than a majority of individuals. Statements like "I'm just one person" or "I can't really make a difference" are pervasive among the reasons people give for disengagement from politics. In a service-learning setting, students can come to understand the importance of being self-starters, taking ownership for their actions, and developing a sense of personal and political efficacy, all dispositions of political participation. For the instructor who wants to make a case for service-learning *and* for political engagement, clarifying this linkage for students like Ann, Michael, and Amy is key to overcoming skepticism and resistance. Moreover, directly eliciting positive outcomes from those students who have already experienced service-learning can be a teachable moment for others who may be resistant and who react to the concept.

6

PRACTICE MAKES IMPERFECT

Service-Learning for Political Engagement as a Window
Into the Challenges of Political Organizing

Katja M. Guenther

E
ducators typically conceptualize service-learning for political engagement as an empowering experience for students. However, service-learning for political engagement can also expose students to the disheartening reality that social change is hard, thereby reducing their sense of efficacy and challenging an instructor's more positive messages about the possibilities of political action. Such was the case for 16 students who, as part of a sociology course focused on social inequalities, worked with a grassroots organization advocating for workers' rights. Students witnessed directly the difficulties of all-volunteer, nonhierarchical models of organizing, as well as the budgetary realities and organizational limitations of small local groups. While most students entered the service-learning site with enthusiasm, they soon reported feeling disheartened, frustrated, and cynical.

Challenging Social Inequalities Through Service-Learning for Political Engagement

In the course Sociology of Social Inequalities, students worked with a small grassroots organization in a city that has some of the state's highest rates of poverty and is home to a large community of service workers or individuals who work in service industries such as domestic and commercial cleaning and lawn care. Most of these workers are from Mexico and Central America, and a significant proportion of them likely do not have valid visas to work in the United States. Marginalized as immigrants and poor, and often additionally at a disadvantage by their status as undocumented workers, these women and men are subject to low wages, typically work in jobs without any kind of health care or other benefits, and are vulnerable to employer abuse.

As a kind of democratic paradox, the county is one of the wealthiest areas of the entire state but has a notoriously weak social service infrastructure leaving workers with few resources. Almost all services are open either to legal residents only or are offered through religious institutions with proselytizing ambitions. Furthermore, most of the state- and church-based social services are limited to the provisioning of food or shelter.

The Western Service Workers Association (WSWA), where students completed service-learning, is one of a few organizations in the area that offers assistance to undocumented workers and a wide range of services and programs beyond trying to meet immediate material needs. WSWA staff distribute food and clothing from a warehouse near their office, located in a quaint single-family home in a residential area near downtown. The organization solicits donations of time and facilities from local physicians and dentists who provide uninsured workers with medical and dental care at low or no cost.

WSWA staff also coordinate social events intended to build community. Conversation groups and formal presentations routinely take place at the headquarters. These meetings increase solidarity and knowledge about labor organizing and serve as arenas where members can make strategic suggestions for campaigns. Members celebrate holidays together and organize special events like a haunted house and dance party at Halloween that many students in this class, Sociology of Social Inequalities, helped to coordinate.

Although service provisioning is a core task at WSWA, the group's primary goal is to organize low-income workers who are not provided union protection or rights under the National Labor Relations Act. To this end, WSWA recruits members to organize campaigns focused on improving the status and rights of service workers.

The organization takes a flexible approach using members' issues as the driving force behind organizing. Few people at WSWA hold positions with titles, no one receives financial compensation, nor is there any type of formalized hierarchy. Instead, WSWA operates as a consensus-driven, nonhierarchical, volunteer-organized group. A small core of volunteers functionally handles WSWA's daily operations—fielding phone calls, coordinating volunteers, facilitating meetings, and soliciting donations. Funding is a constant problem, and given their precarious personal finances, members typically cannot support the organization financially, and the group refuses state funds as a matter of principle.

Service-Learning Course

Participating in service-learning at WSWA presented ample opportunities for students to apply and examine the themes of the course outside the classroom. Students worked on a series of action papers during the semester in which they tied course concepts and readings to their experiences at WSWA with a specific focus on political issues. For example, in one action paper, students assessed the platform of a candidate of their choosing from the presidential primaries and evaluated if and how that candidate's policy proposals would affect WSWA members. Time was also spent in class discussing the challenges facing WSWA and its members, and how those challenges reflected the broader issues the social science literature on social inequalities addresses. Students were exposed to people and situations at WSWA that were new and unfamiliar and challenged their beliefs about social inequalities. Furthermore, students got to see the inner workings of an all-volunteer grassroots organization.

From a more logistical perspective, WSWA was also a practical choice for this service-learning course. WSWA was able to accommodate the full class, which meant students could share their experiences with each other. (I had anticipated some students would object to working with undocumented immigrants and provided the option of other sites for students who were uncomfortable with this population. However, even those students who initially expressed a negative view toward undocumented workers elected to work at WSWA.) An additional logistical advantage was that WSWA's office is open from early in the morning until at least 10:00 p.m. daily, creating ample opportunity for students with complex work and school schedules to find a way to participate.

Preparing Students for Political Engagement

At the start of the semester, I introduced students to the concept of service-learning for political engagement and to the service-learning site. We dedicated a class session to discussing what it means to be politically engaged on issues of social inequality, debating and discussing whether certain activities (e.g., registering voters in poor neighborhoods, organizing a conversation between residents and police about racial profiling, donating to charities serving the homeless) constituted political engagement. My goal was to encourage students to think critically from the outset about what it means to be politically engaged and to recognize and understand different avenues for political engagement (i.e., through institutional or noninstitutional channels or through electoral or informal politics).

Following our in-class discussion of service-learning and political engagement, two representatives from WSWA came to speak to the class. A core staff member, a middle-aged White woman with a background in labor organizing, and an undocumented worker who spoke limited English explained the history of the organization, the problems service workers in the county face, and the types of activities students could engage in with WSWA. The students immediately responded with warmth and enthusiasm, asking a lot of questions about service workers' experiences and appearing quite excited about the service-learning component of the course.

Students primarily worked as canvassers, although a few also spent time soliciting donations from local businesses (specifically for WSWA's food bank), helping with office work, or coordinating a special event. Given that potential members often do not have permanent addresses or working phones, WSWA must engage in active outreach to stay in contact with its potential constituency. Volunteers canvass door to door in teams in neighborhoods with high concentrations of service workers, providing information about WSWA and urging potential members to get involved.

No Spanish, No Money, No Time, No Hope: Students Uncover the Democratic Challenges of Grassroots Organizing

Once students began their service-learning in earnest, many reported an initial discomfort with the door-to-door canvassing, expressing concern about their personal safety (although this activity is always done in teams) and about feeling invasive. Those who could not speak Spanish wondered if the activity was a good use of their time as they often could not communicate effectively with the people they met while canvassing. Students had to confront their own expectations of poor Latinos and Latinas and of cultural miscommunication.

In one of their first action papers students created a collage of dominant images of low-income people of color and service workers and then used course readings to deconstruct these images and discuss how they felt such images influenced their own perceptions of service workers. The paper topic had a powerful effect in encouraging students to evaluate their own assumptions. Upwardly mobile Latino and Latina students, who constituted about 35% of the class, had especially strong reactions because many of them came from households that encouraged them to increase the social distance between themselves and "undesirable" Latinos and Latinas, like service workers. These students at once recognized their parents or grandparents in the service workers but also were eager to move beyond such an image of working poor Latinos and Latinas, in their own minds and in the broader society.

While I had anticipated students might struggle with stereotypes about poor immigrant workers, I had not expected how much students would have internalized the idea that it's impossible to communicate across what they viewed as cultural barriers. Half the students in the class were the children of at least one immigrant parent. Because of the high levels of diversity on campus, I assumed students would have a lot of experience working with people with diverse language competencies. Yet several students had virtually no tolerance for language differences and declared it simply impossible to coordinate groups of people with different language backgrounds. Other students were more willing to rely on nonverbal communication or to struggle with piecemeal Spanish skills. In class we discussed with little agreement to what degree language barriers inhibited organizational success. Students widely concurred that WSWA and similar organizations need to reach out to all people, irrespective of the language they speak, but disagreed strongly on how to do this, with some students advocating for the consistent availability of translators and others advocating for a make-do-with-what-you've-got approach.

Two other challenges about grassroots organizing with Latino and Latina workers soon came to the fore. One was the lack of financial resources. Complaints initially trickled in about longer-term WSWA volunteers asking students for monetary donations. WSWA volunteers had asked me for financial assistance during my meetings with them to set up the service-learning project, but I had not thought to expect this for students. While many students initially responded with extreme negativity about these appeals, what ultimately emerged was that students felt they had greater resources than service workers but still not enough to make a donation that would significantly alter the material realities of WSWA or the people it serves. Some students resented being asked for money outright, but the more common issue was that students couldn't see how the organization could survive on the kinds of small donations it requested, like $10 or $20.

The students' second concern was about the amount of time it would take to effect meaningful social change. Issues of time arose almost immediately. The first problems involving time came in the form of complaints about how late at night WSWA core volunteers would call students. Core volunteers would contact students as late as 11:00 p.m. or midnight, imploring them to come in the next day to assist with a project. When students voiced their complaints about these calls, I asked them why this might be happening. This discussion soon led to the broader recognition of the lack of people's time WSWA had at its disposal. As one student summed up in class, "Desperate situations ask for desperate measures." Most students became increasingly forgiving of appeals on their time but simultaneously became convinced that their contributions of time—like any monetary contributions they could make—were simply insufficient to achieve the kinds of broader social change most of them aspired to effect.

Students in the class perceived diversity and a lack of resources—financial and other—as barriers to successful mobilizations that would catalyze social change. Although some students from the outset of the course recognized the need or value of gradual, incremental change, most wanted to see their actions have an immediate and profound effect. This doesn't mean they expected that we would witness sudden public respect for service workers, an increase in the minimum wage, or a socialist revolution; rather, students wanted to see their work as having a direct human impact, and they didn't see that happening. Instead, what they experienced was feeling like a small drop in a large bucket.

Practice Makes Better: Overcoming Barriers to Political Engagement

To counter a sinking sense of efficacy among the students, we devoted time in class to discussing how entrenched social inequalities may require long, slow, and often trying challenges to shift. To spark this conversation, we read and discussed excerpts from an essay addressing core American myths about social change (Baumgardner & Richards, 2007), for example, that change happens quickly or that one person typically catalyzes social movement success. We also discussed if and how the students' current actions at WSWA could or would contribute to that organization's broader goals of fair labor practices for service workers. Students debated various best-case scenarios, creating and evaluating their dream organization and its outcomes.

Like many educators embarking on service-learning for the first time, I encountered challenges I didn't expect. I anticipated students would struggle with issues of race, ethnicity, and class. I was prepared to address those issues and had ample opportunity to connect students' reactions and observations to our course material on social inequalities. However, students' level of frustration with making change startled me. I was moderately successful in redirecting the class toward productive and relevant conversations about inequalities and social change. Still, I realize retrospectively that I needed to dedicate more time in class, as well as have a greater selection of targeted exercises and readings, to help students grapple with the complexities of political organizing whether in the form of grassroots organizing like WSWA or the formal, institutionalized politics of the presidential primaries, which were under way at the same time. This may have helped students develop and maintain a higher sense of efficacy as well as a more thorough understanding of, and appreciation for, different avenues of political engagement.

Reference

Baumgardner, J., & Richards, A. (2007). Manifesta. In M. L. Andersen & P. Hill Collins (Eds.), *Race, class, and gender: An anthology* (pp. 547–550). Belmont, CA: Thomson Wadsworth.

7

MODELING CITIZENSHIP

The Nexus of Knowledge and Skill

Stephanie Stokamer

I thought that a service-learning course specifically dedicated to social justice was an instructional dream come true. I had visions of students leaving my class inspired and empowered, ready to fight for social justice.
Instead, I found myself struggling to keep my students engaged, and rather
than being prepared for democratic citizenship, the students became disenchanted with the overwhelming complexity of social problems.

The Need for Teaching Civic Skills

Participation is a form of power in a democratic society. Empowerment to
participate and its inherent implications for social justice are tied to foundational thinkers in citizen education such as Dewey, Horton, and Freire (Fox,
2006; Saltmarsh, 1996). Moreover, numerous scholars have articulated components of democratic empowerment. Verba, Schlozman, and Brady (1995),
for example, delineate two main factors in political participation—
motivation and capacity. Kirlin (2003) draws distinctions among civic skills,
normative beliefs, and civic knowledge. Likewise, according to Saltmarsh
(2005), "To engage effectively in the processes of democracy . . . students
will need to acquire, as part of their education, the knowledge, skills, and
values necessary to participate as engaged, democratic citizens" (p. 50). Cress,
Collier, Reitenauer, and Associates (2005) note the application of knowledge
as central to developing the civic capacity necessary for active and effective

citizenship. Similarly, Kirlin (2002) argues that development of civic skills is the salient factor in future civic engagement.

But research has indicated that young people are not likely to participate in civic affairs if they are not confident in their knowledge of democratic principles. Students predictably argue that a person should cast a vote only if he or she is knowledgeable about the candidates and issues, and those who do not fully grasp an issue should stay out of the democratic process. Indeed, many cite their own ignorance as the reason they have not participated in civic affairs. As Kiesa et al. (2007) revealed, "Many students . . . perceive political involvement to be intimidating because it is complicated and they do not feel qualified, they do not know enough" (p. 23).

Civic Knowledge Dilemmas

Informed democratic participation seems a reasonable enough expectation of civic skills and knowledge. However, emphasizing knowledge as a prerequisite to democratic involvement risks leaving students frustrated and disenfranchised by the feeling that they do not know enough to participate. A recent experience in one of my courses illustrates this dilemma.

The significance of understanding empowerment and its role in civic development emerged in a senior-level interdisciplinary service-learning course titled Civic Leadership for Social Change. Using the tools available to most everyday citizens—newspaper articles, film, the Internet, and such—students examine a particular topic (such as social justice, homelessness, or the prison system), and my community partner arranges related service projects. The class is designed to explore ways to create social change through civic involvement.

Nevertheless, such a lofty topic as civic skills for social justice created a civic knowledge dilemma. Provocative films about such topics as gay rights and the treatment of the mentally ill in prison led to lively discussions but were tinged with frustration and body language that indicated discouragement.

Melinda, a former AmeriCorps member, was already sensitive to issues of social justice. According to her early journal reflections, she came into the course eager to take her passion for social change "to the next level" and was excited to learn about "civic leadership." But I was therefore taken aback when two thirds of the way through the academic term Melinda's in-class minute reflection paper revealed that she felt "depressed, disenchanted, and less prepared to create change than when the class began." Numerous other student papers mirrored these sentiments.

Here was my instructional challenge: Students need knowledge to feel confident enough to democratically participate in community issues, but knowledge alone does not necessarily lead to empowerment. In fact, new knowledge can be a kind of Pandora's box—opening up but overwhelming students' minds and emotions.

I had prioritized learning content—empowering through knowledge—over learning specific democratic techniques—empowering through application of knowledge or civic skill. Melinda and her peers were learning difficult material conceptually and psychologically. One cannot teach social justice without pointing to the ways prejudice and complex structural systems contribute to inequalities in our society. Students were overwhelmed with the depth of the problems they were examining and felt disempowered as a result.

Indeed, scholarship has questioned the notion that service-learning builds civic engagement. In an examination of the relationship between service-learning and political engagement, Hunter and Brisbin (2000) found only a limited impact from service on students' political attitudes and behaviors. Kirlin (2002) suggests that "one reason for the weak empirical results relative to civic engagement is that many service and volunteer programs have failed to sufficiently address development of fundamental civic skills such as expressing opinions and working collectively to achieve common interests as part of their design" (p. 571). Kirlin (2003) further asserts that civic skills are developmental in nature and tied to cognitive growth. She suggests that while broad skills such as communication, collective decision making, and critical thinking can be applied to a variety of situations, their use in a civic context is less likely to occur unless specifically practiced in that domain. Likewise, Wang and Jackson (2005) found that students ranked their general support of the importance of civic involvement higher than their own skill level or their individual commitment to it.

Linking civic skill development with civic knowledge enhancement is clearly critical to student empowerment and a worthy objective for service-learning courses. But true democratic empowerment will depend upon how faculty assist students with processing and practicing civic knowledge and skills.

Pedagogical Strategies for Democratic Empowerment

In outlining the synergy between political learning, critical thinking, and reflective judgment, Pascarella and Terenzini write that "purposeful instruction and practice in deliberation about ill-structured problems" contribute to cognitive growth (as cited in Colby, Beaumont, Ehrlich, & Corngold, 2007, p. 57). Cognitive growth can lead to increased civic action when service-learning courses include intentionally designed instructional strategies for merging democratic knowledge and practice (Lee, Olszewski-Kubilius, Donahue, & Weimholt, 2008).

In my service-learning course, I front-loaded civic information under the pedagogical assumption that social justice knowledge would lead to civic skill development as the class moved deeper into service practice. Instead, just the opposite occurred: Cognitive overload debilitated civic skill enhancement.

In unpacking the idea of democratic empowerment for social justice, two fundamental changes have occurred in my service-learning course. First, civic skills are practiced earlier in the term so that civic participation is not just the culmination of learning but a primary source of learning. In week four, students research legislative bills, monitor the activities of their representatives, or sign up to testify before the city council. Performing these civic actions actually helps facilitate processing civic knowledge as students better understand economic, political, and social factors that lead to democratic justice and injustice. It is an instructional form of reflective participation in that knowledge drives civic action, which then becomes a source of further knowledge through reflection.

The second pedagogical shift I have made through integrating multiple activities of reflection and critical analysis (e.g., minute papers, pair-shares, double journal entries) is helping students feel comfortable with the fact that knowledge, like democracy, is messy, imperfect, and always in the making. I highlight how democratic decision making and the challenges of living in civil society are never resolved, and while the specifics might change, issues of crime and punishment, health care, housing, and social justice are a part of our collective learning as a democratic society.

These instructional strategies have resulted in student reports of feeling capable of creating positive community change. Students have said that future democratic participation has become a more tangible process for them as they have become aware of the small contributions they already make, and they now feel more empowered to apply democratic knowledge and skills in rectifying civic and social inequities.

References

Colby, A., Beaumont, E., Ehrlich, T., & Corngold, J. (2007). *Educating for democracy*. San Francisco, CA: Jossey-Bass.

Cress, C. M., Collier, P. J., Reitenauer, V. L., & Associates. (2005). *Learning through serving: A student guidebook for service-learning across the disciplines*. Sterling, VA: Stylus.

Fox, H. (2006). Teaching empowerment. *Michigan Journal of Community Service Learning, 3*(1), 56–61.

Hunter, S., & Brisbin, R. (2000). The impact of service learning on democratic and civic values. *PS: Political Science and Politics, 33*(3), 623–626.

Kiesa, A., Orlowski, A., Levine, P., Both, D., Kirby, E., Lopez, M., et al. (2007). *Millenials talk politics: A study of college student political engagement*. College Park, MD: Center for Information and Research on Civic Learning and Engagement.

Kirlin, M. (2002). Civic skill building: The missing component in service programs? *PS: Political Science and Politics, 35*(3), 571–575.

Kirlin, M. (2003). *The role of civic skills in fostering civic engagement*. Retrieved from http://www.civicyouth.org/circle-working-paper-06-the-role-of-civic-skills-in-foster-civic-engagement/

Lee, S., Olszewski-Kubilius, P., Donahue, R., & Weimholt, K. (2008). The Civic Leadership Institute: A service-learning program for academically gifted youth. *Journal of Advanced Academics, 19*(2), 272–308. Retrieved from http://www.eric.ed.gov/PDFS/EJ794106.pdf

Saltmarsh, J. (1996). Education for critical citizenship: John Dewey's contribution to the pedagogy of service learning. *Michigan Journal of Community Service Learning, 3*(1), 13–21.

Saltmarsh, J. (2005). The civic promise of service learning. *Liberal Education, 91*(2), 50–55.

Verba, S., Schlozman, K., & Brady, H. (1995). *Voice and equality: Civic voluntarism in American politics*. Cambridge, MA: Harvard University Press.

Wang, Y., & Jackson, G. (2005). Forms and dimensions of civic involvement. *Michigan Journal of Community Service Learning, 12*(3), 39–48.

PART THREE

CREATING DEMOCRATIC
LEARNING COMMUNITIES
WITHIN AND WITHOUT

8

CONSENSUS, COLLABORATION, AND COMMUNITY

Mutually Exclusive Ideals?

Christine M. Cress

As Stephanie Stokamer suggests in Chapter 7, modeling citizenship requires teaching and practicing democratic knowledge and skills. Simply reading about democratic processes such as grassroots ballot initiatives or participating in democratic practices such as voting will not necessarily create a nexus for political engagement. Similarly, the creation of learning communities in the classroom and with community partners requires intentional instructor leadership and facilitation. Students' experiences working in groups or participating in team projects may not have always been positive; guidance on how to form, create norms, and perform in collaborative efforts needs to be directly addressed early by service-learning faculty (Collier & Voegele, 2005).

One of the essential differences between service-learning and traditional classrooms is that individuals are no longer isolated subjects. Engagement in service-learning portends that all students are part of the community, or as Reitenauer (2005) explains, it means moving from *I* to *We*. We are the classroom community and we are the local, national, and global community. Service-learning fundamentally resituates a student's social location from knowledge receiver to co-constructor of reality.

Perhaps that is why students can become simultaneously excited and daunted by the prospect of community engagement; making meaningful contributions to the community is hard work. Indeed, community engagement is the quintessential ideal and challenge of democracy: figuring out how to confer the talents and imagination of *I* while acquiescing to and merging with the expertise and vision of *We*. How does an individual balance asserting his or her own cause without overlooking the perspectives and needs of others? How does an individual join the cause of a group without losing a sense of self?

Getting to We

Dirkx (2001) asserts that negotiating the fluid boundaries of *I* and *We* is a constant dilemma whether referring to a family, work group, or classroom community. On a national level, it is the democratic dilemma. How do I protect my individual rights as a patriot *while* recognizing that a requirement of citizenship is the loss of some individual rights for the greater good? In the United States (as in other democratic societies), freedoms of speech and action are constrained within the contexts of community. In classrooms the same is true. Students (and faculty) must restrain their own voices to be inclusive of others.

Cognitively, most students can accept the dualistic contradictions of these competing roles. Perhaps more complex is the inverse relationship: I have a responsibility to and for the welfare of others as a citizen whether or not those others share my views and ways of life. This is the democratic burden we often drop on students through service-learning, a *We* burden of democratic responsibility that can conflict with many White middle-class students' typical meritocratic thinking: *I* get my just rewards for the effort *I* invest. If *I* work hard *I* will receive an A. If *I* volunteer my services in the community, community members will appreciate me.

Service-learning that is project and group based, as opposed to direct service such as tutoring, can further heighten these *I/We* challenges. Whose idea will frame the group project? And what does it mean to receive a group project grade? Moreover, applying and learning new knowledge and skills in unfamiliar environments and often with people of different backgrounds can create psychological and even physical disequilibrium. Students may struggle with finding *We* connections between themselves and these new communities.

Such disruptions have the potential to be teachable moments, but as shown in Chapter 3 and Chapter 11, there is also the potential for students to react negatively to cognitive and sensory overloads. Responses can consist of depressive retreat into oneself, including overindulgence in alcohol and drugs to soothe the dissonant pain, or verbal lashing out and blaming other students, the instructor, the community partner, or community clients.

While not a panacea for avoiding all conflict and miscommunication, intentional course design can set the stage for helping students span these *I/We* border crossings. Three strategies are discussed below: community partnerships, classroom interactions, and cultural preparations and connections.

Community Partnerships

As Judith Liu shows in Chapter 9, cultivating a mutually beneficial reciprocal relationship between the college and the community organization requires advance preparation and sustained attention. Many higher education campuses have centers for service or volunteerism that can facilitate these connections. Often faculty members access these resources and use previously established partnerships rather than initiating new ones. Regardless, it is usually critical for the faculty and community partner to discuss expectations and service-learning parameters prior to class engagement in community activities. While learning and serving are the ultimate goals, there are frequently logistical obstacles to overcome (How will students reach the community site?), legal or health requirements to meet (What safeguards ensure protection of students and the teenage inmates they are tutoring?), and the service roles and responsibilities of students (How many hours per week should students devote and to what type of activities?).

As suggested in Chapter 4, detailing the service experience and connecting it directly to course learning outcomes in the syllabus can serve as a written reference for faculty, students, and community partners. Alternatively, these can be developed as part of a class activity and placed on a class electronic bulletin board during the academic term. Some faculty give students a choice of multiple community partners. Marcia Hernandez describes in Chapter 10 how she invites community partners to class to provide organizational overviews, present community needs, and describe service opportunities. Ironically, what students may end up doing and learning may be different from initial impressions of service sites. Still, allowing students to self-select their site retains the essence of *I* while moving toward *We*.

Class Interactions

Teaching service-learning courses places instructors in new roles and positions. Rather than standing at a lectern each class meeting dispensing facts and information, most faculty engage students as collaborators of learning. Thus, faculty themselves move from *I* as the source of knowledge to *We* as the co-creators of understanding.

This shift is rewarding but difficult. Unfortunately, some faculty swing the educational pendulum too far to *You* the students who are solely responsible for the outcomes. Abdicating teacher accountability from I (teacher) to You (students) can result in a lack of learning and failure in appropriate service. Parker Palmer (1997) in *The Courage to Teach* writes eloquently of transitioning our pedagogical approaches from teaching to learning and moving from *I* the teacher to *We* the co-learners, while dependably maintaining class structures and safeguards. As Palmer iterates, our instructional tasks of guiding, challenging, encouraging, and facilitating should never be fully relinquished or underestimated in educational importance.

Three instructional strategies that can serve students and faculty in clarifying roles and responsibilities are the creation of a classroom intentions list, the development of individual or group service tasks and timelines, and a model of engaged citizenship that can be used to frame assignments and activities.

Classroom intentions. Developing classroom intentions is commonly used in a variety of academic disciplines. During one of the initial class sessions (whether in person or online), students brainstorm a list of words and phrases that describe their ideal classroom interaction. Instructors facilitate this brainstorming by asking questions such as: How should large group discussions be handled? Should I call on students? Should students raise their hands? What if someone is offended by a remark? What about sharing personal or confidential information? What has worked or not worked in previous classes that you do or don't want to happen again? and writing down student responses.

Once the brainstorm list has been generated, instructors then revisit the items and ask for discussion. Who agrees or disagrees with particular ideas? This is also a time for instructors to say how they may or may not insert themselves into the dialogue process. If there is disagreement or conflict, when will the instructor intervene? Or if the instructor makes a statement that is upsetting, how might the instructor like to be made aware of it?

Ultimately, everyone generally agrees to abide by the class intentions list, which is then electronically posted or paper copied for future reference. Essentially, the classroom intentions list helps each member of the class, including the instructor, become part of the *We* of the learning community with its attendant responsibilities.

Action and learning plan for serving (ALPS). The second strategy, depending on the nature of the service activities, is to formulate an individual or group ALPS (see also Reitenauer, Spring, et al., 2005). Creating a spreadsheet with task and timeline categories can help keep all students accountable for their actions. It is also possible to incorporate course learning objectives and other class assignments into these service action plans to facilitate and highlight the linkages between academic content and community activities. At the conclusion of the course, the ALPS can also be reviewed to analyze the relative success of the serving and learning.

A model of engaged citizenship. Finally, a powerful pedagogical model for visually representing the relationship among individual student learning, group interaction, and community action as a form of democratic citizenship is the Social Change Model of Leadership Development (Astin & Astin, 1996). The Social Change Model has three interdependent and dynamic levels characterized by seven *C* words intended to evoke the critical values of the model (see Figure 8.1).

At the individual level are Consciousness of self, Congruence, and Commitment. The premise is that individuals need a clear understanding of their skills and values to behave in ways consistent with their life principles and purpose. As these are clarified, it allows for intentionally co-joining with others.

At the group level are Collaboration, Common purpose, and Controversy with civility. The premise is that groups are formed through finding a common ground of morals, ethics, and ideals toward which to strive. Nevertheless, conflicts are inevitable and can be resolved only through humanity and humility.

This sets the stage for the final level—Community—which emerges from citizenship when the individual and group responsibly connect for the benefit of all in the contexts of difference.

Specific class activities aimed at each level of the Social Change Model can further reinforce connections between individual and group efforts in the context of service-learning and citizenship (see Cress, Collier, Reitenauer, & Associates, 2005). In addition, readings, research, and reflection

FIGURE 8.1
Social Change Model of Leadership Development

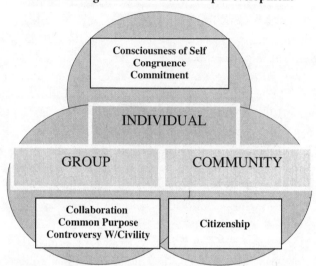

Source: From *A Social Change Model of Leadership Development: Guidebook, Version III*, by A. W. Astin & H. S. Astin, 1996. Los Angeles, CA: Higher Education Research Institute, University of California.

exercises on each of the levels can serve as a critical tool for analyzing individual, organizational, and societal factors that contribute to community problems such as homelessness, truancy, crime, environmental degradation, and lack of health care.

Examining issues through multiple lenses can lead not only to increased critical thinking but to a heightened sense of community consciousness. As opposed to traditional notions of critical thinking where the emphasis is on abstract, logical, and impersonal arguments, students are able to extend their intellectual capacities to include empathy and problem solving that will have a real community impact. In this spirit, service-learning offers students the opportunity to become critically conscious citizens with the knowledge and skills for creating more equitable democratic communities.

Cultural Preparations and Connections

The vast majority of service-learning students enter communities of which they have little knowledge or direct experience. Unfortunately, what they do know may be based on stereotypic perceptions derived from television and other forms of media. A stereotype is a "hardening of the categories," a process of developing rigid ways of thinking about individuals from other cultural backgrounds, as if those individuals represent a statistical norm of their culture group (Reitenauer, Cress, & Bennett 2005). Too often poorly designed and conducted service-learning experiences have served to reinforce negative impressions of the community and its members, although even well-designed service activities can leave students feeling frustrated and frightened if there are not ample opportunities for reflection and perception checking.

Preparing students for community service through cultural self-awareness is the first step toward building intercultural sensitivity and competence. As described earlier, readings, research, and lectures about the history, religious, and ethnic contexts of the community provide important core knowledge.

In Chapter 6, Katja Guenther asks students to create a collage of visual images of low-income people of color and service workers and then use course readings to deconstruct the images and how this influences students' own perceptions of service workers. Becky Boesch in Chapter 14 and Kathleen Yep in Chapter 20 describe additional visual and verbal strategies for getting students to reflect on their own cultural backgrounds, to investigate their own experiences of privilege and disempowerment using course concepts as analysis tools, and to identify potential bridges of connections they may have with their community partners and clients.

Bennett and Bennett (2004) contend that developing intercultural competence requires a *mindset*, a *skillset*, and a *heartset*. Intercultural competence necessitates a *mindset* that is open to learning new knowledge that is embedded with the nuances and contractions of cultures. For instance, what might be considered a lie in one culture—saying, "Yes, I understand" when the individual does not understand—may be considered in another culture as a socially appropriately way to show respect.

Similarly, becoming interculturally competent requires a *skillset* that is adaptable to events and situations. Take the nuances of language, for example. In Hindi, using the correct grammatical phrasing and pronoun agreement when talking to a child is quite different from interacting with a village elder according to Indian cultural customs of hierarchy, honor, and respect. As a further example, a female student in your class may refer to herself as

Chicana rather than Hispanic or Latina. Obviously, the lesson here is to build a proficient *skillset* that integrates individual and cultural contexts.

The third essential component of intercultural competence is a *heartset*, an openness to learning from others, admitting mistakes whether intentional or not, and showing an interest in connecting with the human essence of others.

While these three dimensions of intercultural competence may strike some as rather ethereal, they can be used as a parsimonious approach for teaching and learning construction. To wit, what do students need to *know* about community culture? What do students need to *do* to be effective within community cultural contexts? And, what *attitudes* and dispositions might motivate students and community members alike to engage with one another? In answering these questions, faculty can then identify the specific content, assignments, and activities that are most likely to result in interculturally competent service and learning.

Given the contentious nature of most community issues, not to mention the myriad of variations in personalities and behaviors in and outside the classroom, these strategies are no guarantee that tensions and conflicts will not arise. Indeed, disorienting dilemmas can be valuable sources of learning and meaning-making. Still, the strategies outlined in this chapter can put service-learning planning and processes into relief as a fully democratic experience with all its inherent dilemmas, challenges, and rewards.

References

Astin, A. W., & Astin, H. S. (1996). *A social change model of leadership development: Guidebook, version III.* Higher Education Research Institute, Los Angeles, CA: University of California.

Bennett, J. M., & Bennett, M. J. (2004). Developing intercultural sensitivity: An integrative approach to global and domestic diversity. In D. Landis, J. M. Bennett, & M. J. Bennett (Eds.), *Handbook of intercultural training* (3rd ed., pp. 147–165). Thousand Oaks, CA: Sage.

Collier, P. J. & Voegele, J. (2005). Groups are fun, groups are not fun. In C. M. Cress, P. J. Collier, V. L. Reitenauer, & Associates (Eds.), *Learning through Serving: A student guidebook for service-learning across the disciplines* (pp. 45–66). Sterling, VA: Stylus.

Cress, C. M., Collier, P. J., Reitenauer, V. L., & Associates. (2005). *Learning through serving: A student guidebook for service-learning across the disciplines.* Sterling, VA: Stylus.

Dirkx, J. M. (2001). The power of feelings: Emotion, imagination, and the construction of meaning in adult learning. *New Directions for Adult and Continuing Education, 89,* 63–72.

Palmer, P. J. (1997). *The courage to teach: Exploring the inner landscape of a teacher's life.* San Francisco, CA: Jossey-Bass.

Reitenauer, V. L. (2005). Becoming community: Moving from I to we. In C. M. Cress, P. J. Collier, V. L. Reitenauer, & Associates (Eds.), *Learning through serving: A student guidebook for service-learning across the disciplines* (pp. 33–44). Sterling, VA: Stylus.

Reitenauer, V. L., Cress, C. M., & Bennett, J. (2005). Creating cultural connections: Navigating difference, investigating power, unpacking privilege. In C. M. Cress, P. J. Collier, V. L. Reitenauer, & Associates (Eds.), *Learning through serving: A student guidebook for service-learning across the disciplines* (pp. 67–82). Sterling, VA: Stylus.

Reitenauer, V. L., Spring, A., Kecskes, K., Kerrigan, S. M., Cress, C. M., & Collier, P. J. (2005). Building and maintaining community partnerships. In C. M. Cress, P. J. Collier, V. L. Reitenauer, & Associates (Eds.), *Learning through serving: A student guidebook for service-learning across the disciplines* (pp. 17–32). Sterling, VA: Stylus.

9

CULTIVATING RELATIONSHIPS BETWEEN A GRASSROOTS ORGANIZATION AND A UNIVERSITY

Judith Liu

While a course like Political Sociology during a presidential election year would appear to be an easy fit for implementing a service-learning component, the task was far from simple because the political component had to be nonpartisan, and the community partner had to provide a sociological context for students' understanding of politics and power.

Now in its 30th year, the San Diego Organizing Project (SDOP) is a faith-based organization that includes 29 Christian congregations. SDOP works with individual congregations to develop their own community organizing plans. Coordinators are assigned to work with designated congregations that in turn create their own organizing ministries on issues such as youth dropout rates, gang violence, or the lack of after-school activities. Typically, the organizing ministries invite resource holders (such as council members, church and community leaders, law enforcement officials, and the mayor) to a community action event to hear concerns about youth needs in the community. After the meeting a citywide Youth Convention is scheduled followed by a Get-Out-the-Vote Campaign.

SDOP was a good community partner choice because it already had well-established roots in the community, ties with our university, and a history of successful results. Student teams could work with organizing ministries to facilitate for their own plans, and the class could help with the Youth Convention.

Obstacles to Community-University Collaboration

Despite existing connections, however, any community-university collaboration can face obstacles that range from differences in operating schedules between academic calendars and the community organizations' fiscal calendars to helping students become prepared for interacting with new community populations. Also, grassroots organizations can be so deeply implanted in a community that organizers may have difficulty seeing alternate ways of operating. Even in our case, SDOP officials had reservations about students working in their field of influence.

Steps for Unifying University and Community

I initiated a meeting with the SDOP director 9 months prior to the service-learning course. During our meeting we discussed mutual expectations and trepidations about the collaboration. My goal was to build our relationship through monthly telephone and e-mail communications. Yet six months later, I still had not heard anything more. As a strategy for obtaining more concrete information to include in the course syllabus and to get a better understanding of how SDOP operated, I also attended a full-day training session for the organizing ministries.

At the training session I was introduced to SDOP congregations, and several key members in those congregations expressed interest in having college students work with them. Having a better understanding of SDOP's history, mission, and purpose, I drafted my syllabus and met again with the director. I explained how the syllabus was a vital tool for organizing the course, and together we mutually revised it. This assisted SDOP members with understanding the dynamics of a college service-learning course, and in turn I learned about the exigencies of organizations that are perennially shorthanded and underfunded and whose own efforts are frequently dictated by the schedules of others.

Even with the best of intentions, however, the service-learning course was into its fifth week of the semester before congregations were selected by

SDOP and the service-learning activities were finalized. In the interim, students had rightly nagged me for more details about the service activities required for the course. My response to students was: "Democracy is messy. Civic engagement and social responsibility require flexibility and the ability to deal with ambiguity." Secretly, though, I had approached our director of community service learning about possibly severing ties with SDOP and considered other community sites as a contingency plan.

Once service activities were formally identified, I invited SDOP members to the class to provide students with an orientation to its history, purpose, and activities. Involving representatives of SDOP in the classroom helped decrease the power differential that normally exists between campus-community partnerships by letting the community partner speak on its own behalf about expectations. SDOP staff also provided on-site orientations that helped create strong congregation-student team bonds.

Engaging in Collaborative Activities

To help students understand the SDOP organizing process, they were all required to attend one community action meeting prior to working with their partner congregation. While each team of students made arrangements with their own congregations, most teams promoted the Youth Convention by distributing flyers after Sunday services or canvassing the neighborhood surrounding the church. In addition, I attended all required student events as well as any event held at the various congregations throughout the semester. My participation not only demonstrated my commitment to grassroots political involvement, but it also strengthened my relationship with SDOP staff and its organizing ministries. Moreover, it gave me direct insight into student experiences, allowing me to better facilitate in-class discussions and reflections as we made connections between sociological processes and democratic practices.

The Youth Convention was highly successful in its outcomes and in bonding student teams with their congregations, but as was evident in my earlier dealings with SDOP, I had to prod the members to get the students' tasks finalized just days before the event. Students also participated in the Get-Out-the-Vote Campaign by registering voters, distributing flyers on ballot propositions, and participating in a voter reminder phone bank. On election night, the class met to watch and process results from around the county and country. After the election, we used the remainder of the semester to reflect on and analyze the election results in light of sociological forces (e.g., poverty, race, gender) and their impact on democratic processes.

As a consequence of cultivating the relationship with SDOP, I was able to utilize the group as a community partner the following semester for a sociology course that also focused on community concerns. Nurturing a strong grassroots-university connection requires building strong community relationships based on trust, constant communication, collaboration on key elements, and engagement in multiple activities. Together, these strategies yielded a meaningful and genuine partnership.

10

NEGOTIATING STUDENT EXPECTATIONS AND INTERPRETATIONS OF SERVICE-LEARNING

Marcia Hernandez

Previous experience has taught me that most students in Sex and Gender, an undergraduate elective sociology course, are a self-selected group personally interested in the course themes. The students are usually active in campus organizations and often already connected to local community groups through service activities. They tend to be very aware of social inequalities and genuinely want to learn about social movements and strategies to counter discrimination and address inequities. Thus, I assumed I would have a receptive audience to service-learning for increased political engagement as a new course learning objective. However, while service-learning was warmly received by students, different interpretations of what counts as political engagement and how and which type of service should connect to formal learning experiences quickly became apparent.

After querying community organizations to learn how students might benefit the groups through service-learning activities, what new experiences students might gain, and to provide them with the parameters of my service-learning requirements, I decided to form partnerships with a local food bank and a chapter of the League of Women Voters. The two sites represented contrasting positions of political engagement and provided students with a context to observe how political resources are acquired and used by different groups, including the sociological dimensions of gender, race, and social class in local political actions.

I invited representatives from the League and the Food Bank early in the semester to provide the class with information about the two organizations and explain the service-learning opportunities. Student expectations for learning and their interpretations about serving were evident from these initial encounters. The Food Bank representative, Julie, was enthusiastically welcomed. Students asked questions about how much food was distributed and if they could bring other students to work at the organization. Julie is a recent alumna and spoke with a casual and familiar tone. She explained that students would distribute food and stock the warehouse and could organize a campus food drive. Julie emphasized the wide range of people who use the agency's services from working class and the poor to middle-class families who have been affected by the economy's decline.

In contrast, the League representative, Linda, provided a different visual model of educational status, age, and experience. She holds a master's degree, is nearing retirement, and is well known in political circles, having served for decades on various community boards. Linda arrived a few minutes before class began, normally a time when students are animated and talkative. Her arrival silenced the crowd. As she eloquently spoke about the history of the League and the activities of the local chapter I heard a student sitting nearby say to a friend, "She reminds me of my aunt. Look at her scarf!"

The League's service-learning activities were different from those of the Food Bank. Students were required to deal specifically with the political system through a voter registration drive or assisting with a televised candidates' forum or conducting interviews of local chapter members in terms of their personal experiences in political engagement. At the end of Linda's presentation, none of the students had questions about the League or the service-learning activities. Indeed, after she left, students actively resisted partnering with the League.

The student who remarked that Linda looked like her aunt said the League was not an appropriate community partner for service-learning because while its work was beneficial to society, she believed "they don't need help." Other students chimed in that service to the Food Bank would do the most good.

I found this perspective perplexing and sociologically intriguing. I specifically sought organizations whose mission and goals would discourage students from thinking about service-learning "as a form of altruism and charity rather than civic responsibility . . . [that fails] to develop a conception of citizenship grounded in social obligation [and] perpetuates notions of atomistic individualism" (Cook, 2008, p. 6). But clearly it was the experience of charity and the altruism of helping people who were at a disadvantage or in some way different that many of the students wanted and expected in a service-learning class. Although students did become partners with the League, few initially wanted to work with someone who reminded them of a well-educated older family member.

Student resistance to service-learning also appeared in writing assignments. Students were required to keep a journal detailing their service-learning work. The first journal prompt asked students to consider the importance of including service-learning for political engagement in the Sex and Gender course. The entry was due following a class discussion regarding the significance of developing a sociological imagination (Mills, 1959), the concept of responsibility (Heimer & Staffen, 1998), and the community partners' presentations to the class. In spite of course material highlighting the role of gender in social institutions such as politics and education as well as public policy decisions and civil rights, many students did not make a connection between the League and political engagement.

Sarah's journal entry highlights the incongruence some students felt about working with the League and doing service-learning:

> My initial thought on working with a service-learning partner for a Sex and Gender course was that I could not possibly see what service learning had to do with the course. I found myself wondering what the organizations chosen could teach us about sex and gender. I felt they were *more centered on poverty issues and voting and voting rights issues, not so much sex and gender* [emphasis added].

Reframing Service and Campus-Community Connections

I had to emphatically explain to students that the League of Women Voters was an appropriate fit for the Sex and Gender course. The League has historical roots in fighting for political rights and is committed to empowering women (although men are members and can be officers). Today, the League focuses on a variety of issues, including the environment and immigration, that college students also champion.

Despite my best efforts to facilitate service-learning, through class discussions and individual conversations I came to understand that students defined "doing service" as "doing charity." Linda's appearance, behavior, and dress signaled to students that the League of Women Voters did not need assistance, or at least did not need their service as desperately as the Food Bank. Janet, echoing other student concerns, stated, "The League does not need my help as much as the Food Bank does, and I doubt I will learn anything by working with them."

I tried to reframe possible service-learning outcomes, asserting that students could have just as valuable an experience working with the League as the Food Bank. I explained the immeasurable, often invisible ways the League affects a community through voter registration drives or impartial information provided in its publication *Smart Voter*. Ironically, the success of the League in the formal political system and the distinctly political nature of the League's work seemed a deterrent to students' willingness to work with the group. In the end, I convinced and cajoled a few students to work with the League.

Revised Impressions of Service and Community Action

At the end of the semester, students reported to the class about the success and challenges of doing service-learning. Overwhelmingly, students who interviewed League members about their personal stories of political engagement had the most positive experience. The interviews provided students with an opportunity to learn how League members practice what they preach in terms of individual and collective responsibility to their communities.

Kelly reported, "I was amazed at learning how much I did not know. [The interviews] made us aware of how unaware we were."

Another student stated that the League members' "level of civic engagement was above and beyond simply volunteering their time for issues that pertain to the League. . . . For these women civic engagement is a lifestyle."

Students who worked with the Food Bank reported learning important lessons about being involved "to make a difference" and the need to be "an informed citizen when it comes to voting about different policies or for politicians" particularly in light of recent economic trends.

But by the end of the class there was a distinct difference in how each group viewed the service-learning experience. Students who worked with the Food Bank described feeling pessimistic and depressed by the enormity of issues confronting the organization and its clients. In contrast, students who worked with the League felt inspired by women who became role models of the power of an individual's political action.

Some of the students who partnered with the Food Bank expressed a desire to work *for a cause or an issue,* while students who worked with the League approached the service-learning project as *working with a group.* Psychologically and sociologically there is a distinct difference between working for a cause but not feeling connected to the people who may benefit from the work, and working with a group to achieve a goal. Students who worked with the Food Bank were able to perform good deeds, but the extent of social problems related to clients' seeking the Food Bank's assistance left them without a clearly viable political solution for how their being politically engaged could address hunger and poverty.

Service-learning engagement with the League was also more tangibly defined. Projects were clearly outlined at the outset, were relatively short, and had a fixed schedule (such as staffing a table for voter registration at Earth Day or conducting an interview). Students experienced firsthand how one individual act can make a lasting difference for increasing political engagement, such as voter registration. By interviewing League members, students learned that individuals who join organizations could be a powerful force for change in society.

I realized in hindsight that even those students who seem more politically astute and aware of social inequities may need assistance in overcoming their own sociological categorizations of people and organizations. Clarifying and revisiting service-learning definitions, expectations, and interpretations throughout the course are necessary pedagogical requirements for successfully connecting campus and community action for social change.

References

Cook, C. (2008). Beyond service: Community based research and political engagement. In S. C. Tannenbaum (Ed.), *Research, advocacy and political engagement: Multidisciplinary perspectives through service learning* (pp. 3–22). Sterling, VA: Stylus.

Heimer, C. A., & Staffen, L. R. (1998). *For the sake of the children: The social organization of responsibility in the hospital and the home.* Chicago, IL: University of Chicago Press.

Mills, C. W. (1959). *The sociological imagination.* New York, NY: Oxford University Press.

11

SERVICE-LEARNING IS LIKE LEARNING TO WALK

Baby Steps to Cultural Competence

Tanya Renner, RaeLyn Axlund, Lucero Topete,
and Molli K. Fleming

I t's June, a hot and sunny time in Oaxaca, Mexico, with frequent but
brief intense showers in the afternoon, sometimes with thunder and
lightning. Four colleagues from four colleges with differing cultural
backgrounds and experiences are sitting on the airy patio of a local restaurant
enjoying the unique and delightful Oaxacan ambience. We discuss our students who come here from all over the world to study the Spanish language
and Oaxacan culture as well as the hundreds of tiny municipalities representing multiple indigenous villages that make up the state.

Here in the state capital, we appreciate the delights of the crafts for sale
in the streets, sample the unique and delicious cuisine, and tackle the cultural
dilemmas and challenges involved in helping our international service-
learning students to have positive and beneficial experiences. How, for
instance, can we help American students understand that their normal bath-
ing routines in their homestay severely deplete the local water supply? How
can we help students become enriched by service-learning experiences that
do not meet their cultural expectations, especially when many spend significant amounts of money to travel here to learn and serve?

Cultural Perspectives on Service

Lucero's Experiences

For over two decades, service-learning has been nurtured by the faculty and staff of a small, private higher education institution that provides instruction and training in the Spanish language and Mexican culture, the Instituto Cultural Oaxaca (ICO), where Lucero Topete is the director. From Lucero's perspective, service-learning experiences usually work out well for those students who come for 3 months or longer, who are graduate students, or who expect to spend a great deal of time learning the culture and becoming fluent in the language. In contrast, lower-division college students who come for 2 to 8 weeks and have little background in the language and culture are more likely to have unrealistic expectations of what can be accomplished.

In Mexican culture, community service is an everyday, ordinary event. Many Mexican high school students need to get a letter documenting their service (500 hours) before they can receive a diploma, and all public universities require 1 year of service (480 hours). Because there is such an abundance of student help, international service-learners' contributions are not considered special. Students are not praised for doing service any more than they would be for attending school. A student is expected to show up on time and be quietly unobtrusive until needed to carry out a task. The agency the students work with is likely to give students the less desirable tasks that facilitate the work of trained employees. For example, a student might help a service agency by making copies, typing, filing, purchasing supplies, staying in the office when no one else is present, and going to buy a soda or coffee for the director or other office staff. There may also be interesting projects to carry out, with the possibility of additional responsibility for any number of functions. This is most likely to happen if the student is engaged in applying academic knowledge in pursuit of practical experience needed for career preparation.

For young college students from other countries where students' providing service is not as common, the lack of praise and recognition for civic engagement can be seen by these students as strange and unwelcoming. From the perspective of ICO staff, students from some cultures, such as the United States, expect everything to be ready when they arrive, want to make important contributions, and expect to have their service treated as valuable. But generally it is not the responsibility of agency staff in Oaxaca to be concerned with whether students benefit from performing tasks. In this case cultural values of service are at odds, which can create significant misunderstandings and frustration for all involved.

Another issue is that the unique and deeply varied cultural mix of peoples in Oaxaca results in a complex set of social systems and norms. When international service-learning students arrive with little knowledge of the Oaxacan language and culture, it is difficult for students to perceive Oaxacan ways of life and to adapt their service-learning experience accordingly. As such, students don't understand the rhythm of the culture, perceptions of time, or how goals are achieved.

Because it is not uncommon for international service-learning students to be young and idealistic, guiding their service-learning is like helping a child learn to walk: It requires baby steps. Students simply cannot learn Spanish and save the world in 15 days. At times students have complained that their service work is boring or that their skills could be better utilized elsewhere. For some students the services that are truly needed in the community, such as painting houses or teaching English to vendors so they can better communicate with foreign customers, don't seem important. Some students have wanted to work at poor villages without understanding how their behaviors might affect the villagers. For instance, if they were to eat a sandwich in front of villagers who barely have enough to eat, it wouldn't just be rude, it would be a painful scene for the half-starved villagers to witness. In addition, because international students cannot eat the food or drink the water in the poorest villages, working there is just not an option. Students come with varied expectations, such as working in lawyers' offices or in medical clinics or with village healers or midwives. ICO is happy to arrange visits and contacts in the community for these students, but unless they are already licensed, they cannot work as doctors, for example. And the local healers cannot teach a student about their complex and extensive procedures and medicinal products in just a few weeks. Primary challenges, then, include adjusting expectations and helping students take baby steps in obtaining a more realistic understanding of the impact and context of their service efforts.

Molli's Experiences

When Molli Fleming, professor of Spanish at Maui College in Hawaii, brings students for the first time to Oaxaca, most are enthusiastic and willing to adapt. However, our experiences have been consistent with Hammer's

(2005) research regarding the emotional changes and stages of development of someone who lands fresh in a new country and needs to navigate a new language, a homestay family, different surroundings, and unfamiliar food. Initially, there is a predictable sense of great energy and ability, caused in part by adrenaline and other chemicals the body produces to help cope with stressors. After the initial boost of energy is lost, a variety of coping strategies emerge that can be successful but also debilitating.

Some students express frustration with the cultural differences and mis-understandings. Some students simply feel overwhelmed with the language demands. Some become depressed and miss family and partners. Some over-use alcohol to self-medicate their complicated emotions. Some become sick from the food or water. In addition, if a student's appearance is dissimilar from that of local people, the curious stares may result in psychological discomfort.

To complicate matters further, what may start out as a form of social support in the students' service group can become destructive. Students can infect one another with their negativity, for example. Intervention by the director at this point is critical in coaching students on ways to cope and stay open and positive.

Students who are in the country for a short time (1 month or less) never really get a chance to reach their full mental-emotional balance in the culture. There is simply too much to learn and not enough time to acclimate. In effect, students who arrive with the best of intentions and a sense of pur-pose may find themselves struggling to cope with the basics of living and daily language interactions. According to Maslow's (1948) theory of motiva-tion, students will likely focus on basic physiological levels and safety needs. Their actions may appear to be selfish as they struggle to survive. Students who remain in the country longer have a chance to stabilize their basic needs. Thus, according to Maslow's analysis of motivation, they become able to function at higher cognitive, psychological, and emotional levels, such as developing a sense of belonging and feeling good about themselves in new cultural contexts. Engaging in service-learning activities before students can function at these higher levels can add to student stress rather than provide an effective service-learning experience.

Steps to Culturally Competent Service-Learning

Many former international service-learning students expressed years later that their experiences in Oaxaca changed them forever. Understanding the transformative power of a well-balanced international service-learning experience has inspired us to work toward creating more beneficial and constructive opportunities for all our students. We identified three strategic steps for helping students walk toward culturally competent and richer experiences:

1. Develop stronger service-learning program infrastructure and community partnerships.
2. Create an extended orientation for adjusting student expectations and providing Oaxacan-specific cultural training.
3. Maximize service opportunities drawing upon students' strengths, especially their knowledge of English, and their ability to interact with children.

First, developing a stronger infrastructure for this particular program included the identification of a dedicated on-site service-learning coordinator who works with students prior to and during their cross-cultural service experiences, and continues to develop and maintain reciprocal relationships with community partners.

Second, an extended and intensive orientation focuses on increasing students' knowledge of Oaxacan history, culture, and politics; awareness of their own cultures, perspectives, expectations, assumptions, and biases; the understanding of what service-learning means in an Oaxacan context; and the capacity for critical reflection on issues such as intercultural relations, social structures, power, and privilege. Building on Simonelli, Earle, and Story's (2004) recommendations for international service-learning practitioners, the orientation needs to educate students about Mexican views of service, and guide them toward questioning their own conceptions of service and defining it within the context of Oaxacan culture and needs.

The orientation should be further informed by Kiely's (2005) conceptual framework for service-learning as a transformational learning process. Students will participate in dialogues that bring to the surface diverse perspectives and worldviews to help foster awareness of assumptions and facilitate reframing of their own perspectives. Increasing students' intercultural sensitivity will be assisted through regular, structured, critical reflection. Reflection is "the process that helps students connect what they observe and experience in the community with their academic study" (Eyler, 2001, p. 35). In addition, students will explore expectations and goals of the community and how their service might affect the host community (Urraca, Ledoux, & Harris, 2009).

Finally, maximizing students' strengths involves limiting service opportunities to a set number of options with appropriate structure and support. Trying to match students' interests to an endless range of service opportunities is not logistically productive, and their interests often do not match their readiness to engage in the culture and language. Instead, students can choose from two or three options with a structured schedule. This strategy strikes a compromise between community needs and student availability. One example is working with Casa Canica, an educational program for the children of the vendors (mostly women) in a large open-air market in the city. Many of these children do not have other family members who can care for them and there are not enough schools to serve children all day. Service-learning students can assist with homework, tutor in English, and provide structured play.

Final Reflections

In our (and our students') eagerness to be of service in communities, towns, and villages other than our own, we may be likely to run headlong into service opportunities without stopping to reflect on whether we have walked headlong into cultural gateways and trod upon culturally sacred landscapes. Effective service-learning, whether domestic or international, is dependent upon mutual paths of discovery and learning as we take baby steps toward cultural understanding.

References

Eyler, J. (2001). Creating your reflection map. *New Directions for Higher Education, 14*, 35–43.

Kiely, R. (2005). A transformative learning model for service-learning: A longitudinal case study. *Michigan Journal of Community Service Learning, 12*(1), 5–22.

Hammer, M. R. (2005). *Assessment of the impact of the AFS Study Abroad experience.* Retrieved from http://74.52.0.194/downloads/files/assessment.pdf

Maslow, A. H. (1948). Some theoretical consequences of basic need-gratification. *Journal of Personality, 16*(4), 402–416.

Simonelli, J., Earle, D., & Story, E. (2004). Acompanar obedeciendo: Learning to help in collaboration with Zapatista communities. *Michigan Journal of Community Service Learning, 10*(3), 44–56.

Urraca, B., Ledoux, M., & Harris, J. T. (2009). Beyond the comfort zone: Lessons of intercultural service. *The Clearing House, 82*(6), 281–289.

PART FOUR

DECONSTRUCTING DILEMMAS FOR DEMOCRATICALLY CENTERED LEARNING

12

CONFLICT AS A CONSTRUCTIVE CURRICULAR STRATEGY

David M. Donahue

I n the film *A Single Man* (Ford, 2009), the main character, a professor of English during the early 1960s, delivers an impromptu lecture about fear of difference and the way politicians, corporations, and others in power take advantage of such fear for their own ends. In the lecture scene not one student discusses these ideas with others in class and not one disagrees with or raises a question about these provocative remarks. For faculty teaching in college and university classrooms today, particularly those committed to service-learning and democratic education, such scenes seem foreign to thinking about classrooms as places where understanding is not silently received and where talk and disagreement, even uncomfortably contentious talk and disagreement, are considered tools for learning.

Disagreement and disequilibrium and contention and conflict in the classroom are valuable because they are inherent elements in democratic life. Democracy, like the classroom where students are actively engaged in examining ideas about real issues and building their own understanding, can be acrimonious. While some commentators and many citizens bemoan partisanship and the sharp elbows of politics, political conflict is as old as the nation itself. Politics and conflict can also be framed as an opportunity to engage with others, examine new ideas and perspectives, and challenge one's own assumptions, even if that is not always the approach taken by politicians, organizers, bloggers, and opinion writers where winning and shouting louder than others can take precedence over consideration and open-mindedness.

If faculty think of classrooms as places where students are prepared for engaging in the inherent conflict and messiness of political life, they need to frame disagreement as opportunities to learn, not opportunities to win over others. They need to prepare students for value-laden, conflict-ridden situations with tools that allow them to engage, learn, and take action. The rest of this chapter outlines some of the ways to accomplish this and introduces teaching cases by Kathleen Yep, Becky Boesch, and Thomas Van Cleave showing what this looks like in diverse college and university settings.

This chapter begins with a description of Dewey's (1938) notions of continuity and interaction as criteria for thinking about the difference between negative, or miseducative, and positive aspects of conflict, or conflict as a source of learning and motivation to continue engaging with others. It also describes strategies that allow conflict to be productive rather than destructive in learning and democratic engagement and addresses ways to diminish the negative aspects of conflict, particularly where differences of opinion coincide with stereotyped ideas about identity like race, class, religion, or sexual orientation. In considering strategies to address conflict, this chapter highlights the importance and difficulty of modeling for our students how to engage in conflict ourselves, even when—and perhaps especially when—contentious issues are difficult for us to manage.

Continuity, Interaction, and Learning From Conflict

John Dewey (1938) describes two conditions for learning—continuity and interaction—that are useful for thinking about whether and how conflict in a classroom can serve learning. Continuity refers to whether an experience leads to more experiences that promote growth or learning. Of course all experiences can lead to some kind of growth or learning, but some kinds of learning are more worthwhile than others. Dewey notes that one may grow as a burglar, gangster, or corrupt politician. He continues,

> From the standpoint of growth as education and education as growth, the question is whether growth in this direction promotes or retards growth in general. Does this form of growth create conditions for further growth or does it set up conditions that shut off the person who has grown in this particular direction from the occasions, stimuli, and opportunities for continuing growth in new directions? (p. 36)

Because growth is not only intellectual but also moral, growing as a corrupt politician does not exemplify continuity. Such growth represents shutting off oneself from opportunities for growth in new and individually and particularly socially productive directions. By contrast, an experience can be considered productive or contributing to growth if it "arouses curiosity, strengthens initiative, and sets up desires and purposes that are sufficiently intense to carry a person over dead places in the future" (p. 38).

Interaction is the second criterion contributing to growth or learning. Dewey (1938) wrote, "An experience is always what it is because of a transaction taking place between an individual and what, at the time, constitutes his environment" (p. 43). For those of us teaching in colleges and universities, that environment is our classroom, and the important interactions are the ones our students have with each other and with us. As faculty consider whether their classrooms are places for growth and learning, they should consider whether they are promoting interaction as a key constitutive component of learning, or whether, like the professor in *A Single Man*, their classroom is a place operating on a different conception of learning, one that Paulo Freire (1970) labeled the *banking model*, where knowledge is deposited by faculty for future use by students as opposed to a place where, through social interaction, students construct knowledge (Vygotsky, 1978).

Conflict in the Classroom: When It Is Productive

Conflict in the classroom is inevitable. In fact, given the rich, relevant, and provocative content of many college courses, it is noteworthy that classrooms are most often devoid of conflict. This lack of conflict might reflect a lack of continuity or a lack of interaction, conditions that ultimately mean a lack of learning. The job of instructors then is to think about how conflict—intentional or not—can serve continuity and interaction and, ultimately, growth or learning. Especially in service-learning courses where multiple points of view are valued and the teacher does not have total control but shares it with community partners and students, diversity of ideas and conflicting opinions should be expected. As students engage in reflection on service, particularly as they examine issues related to causes of inequity and injustice or political solutions to social problems, conflict is not only inevitable, it can be a prime opportunity for learning.

For example, students reflecting on their service of tutoring young people in an after-school program may disagree on the causes of the achievement gap and the mix of personal and social responsibility in addressing that gap. They may disagree also on whether legislation such as the No Child Left Behind

Act of 2001 is part of the solution or part of the problem. These kinds of classroom disagreements can be productive. They reflect the disagreements that exist in the larger society and represent different philosophical and political worldviews with which students must contend. Managing such differences in opinion with an appreciation for inquiry and respect for others is the work of preparing for democracy where conflict is also inevitable. While many classrooms have rules or norms for talking, learning norms for listening to those one disagrees with fosters a democratic disposition serving a lifetime of openness and dialogue across differences. When students learn to listen to others, consider multiple viewpoints, and inquire into the basis for thinking that differs from their own, they are benefiting from interaction with others. They are also benefiting from situations that contribute to continuity, to a desire to learn more, and to understanding why others think differently. When students are generous to others' ideas, they set up conditions for further interactions with others and continuity in their own and others' learning.

For faculty leading service-learning classrooms, promoting continuity and interaction for learning from conflict means, first, understanding and managing one's self and, second, understanding and managing classroom dynamics. In regard to one's self, while instructors personally hold deeply to their own views, they also want students to develop their own well-articulated and well-defended points of view. Faculty recognize that such points of view may well vary from their own. That said, hearing opinions different from one's own, particularly when they are not well thought out or are insensitive or lacking in generosity to the experiences of others can be difficult, as Yep describes in Chapter 13. Faculty need to recognize these situations and remember to model thoughtful dialogue and also model how to examine controversial issues in ways leading to growth through continuity and interaction. They can ask students to say more. They can ask them to draw on the subject matter of the course to deepen understanding. They can ask questions that help students revisit their thinking or strengthen their arguments. They can say, "I hadn't considered that perspective," and demonstrate flexibility and open-mindedness in their own thinking. They can also work with colleagues who represent different opinions, experiences, and identities to share the responsibility of facilitating classroom dialogue and how they communicate across differences.

Managing one's self has its own set of challenges. Managing a seminar of 12, a classroom of 30, or a lecture hall of 150 has different sets. In some cases, especially in larger classes, not only is conflict absent but so is any student-to-student interaction. In such cases, the instructor may need to foster interaction and even instigate conflict or disequilibrium. While lecture halls present obstacles to interaction, students can talk with someone next to them for one or two minutes at key points during a lecture to connect information from the class to political thought and action. Such conversations allow students to interact with course content and can potentially shake their assumptions about self and others.

Faculty, as Boesch describes in Chapter 14, may also find unexamined uniformity of opinion in their classrooms. In such cases, conflict and its beneficial potential to promote further reflection leading to continuity of learning happens only when faculty instigate it. This faculty responsibility is important not only in classrooms where homogeneity exists but in diverse classrooms where only those holding one point of view or representing one set of experiences dominate classroom discussions.

In smaller classes, faculty may instigate useful conflict through dialogue and interaction by asking students to reflect first on their experiences before sharing them with others. For example, faculty may ask students to develop cases based on their service-learning experiences. Framing and writing a case requires a level of reflection and forethought that might not be present in a free-flowing class discussion without such preparation. Cases allow students to examine their own experience as a text, to step back from experience, and to hear how others read such texts. Faculty can also suggest protocols for reading cases. One protocol requires students to present their case, answer clarifying questions from others, and then listen without comment as others discuss the values and alternative framings they see in the case. The presenting student then has the final word about what he or she learned by listening to a variety of opinions and readings. As the example of cases illustrates, asking students to think ahead of time and listen to others with an open mind makes conflict or disequilibrium that grows out of differences in discussing value-laden situations generative and productive of further growth and continuity of learning.

Conflict in the Classroom: When It Is Unproductive

Even with the best of instructor scaffolding, conflict in the classroom can sometimes be personal, uninformed, and counterproductive. Less useful conflict results, as Yep points out in Chapter 13, when students share unexamined opinions, seek to blame, or make broad generalizations based on stereotypes and limited information. These kinds of conflict are miseducative, leading to student learning that is counter to faculty goals. In miseducative scenarios, students shut down rather than participate. They become defensive rather than open. They see conflict and difference as something to be avoided rather than as something of potential benefit. In other words, unproductive conflict leads to discontinuity of learning and no interaction—two unproductive yet related outcomes.

When miseducative conflict occurs, the faculty member's responsibility is to ameliorate it. First, instructors should name and identify the tension rather than ignore it and hope it goes away. It will not! Not only does ignoring the negative conflict promote more classroom negativity such as physically and cognitively withdrawing, it sets a bad model of interaction, of how to respond to uninformed thinking and thoughtless comments. In such situations, faculty should challenge students' assumptions. Two good questions are: "What do you mean?" and "How do you know that?" When faculty respond this way, they take the burden away from students who may have felt attacked or compelled to defend themselves or a community with which they identify. Faculty also need to provide factual information when students trade in stereotypes or misinformation.

Responding with questions also turns difference and conflict into an opportunity for further inquiry or continued positive growth, a stance represented by the following chapters in this section. Inquiry means asking good questions about phenomena, not rushing to generalizations. It means moving from only a personal stance on a situation to a stance that also includes analysis. Asking students to respond to further questions for reflection also slows down the conversation, allowing for more thoughtfulness and open-mindedness. This is especially true for written reflection. Yep demonstrates in Chapter 13 how this strategy moves a classroom from offensive talk and unformed thinking to nonviolent communication across differences and to a deeper analysis of controversial issues.

Strategies to Promote Productive Reflection, Dialogue, and Conflict

Dewey (1938) wrote that instructors "should know how to utilize the surroundings, physical and social, that exist so as to extract from them all that they have to contribute to building up experiences that are worthwhile"

(p. 40). The following strategies are designed to make conflict productive and therefore worthwhile. Service-learning instructors are at an advantage in creating environments for worthwhile learning because the pedagogy demands reflection from students. Reflection, especially reflection on carefully framed controversial issues before engaging in dialogue, makes discussion amid differing worldviews and political philosophies productive. Consider trying these strategies.

Move away from reliance on whole-group discussions. Whole-group discussions can provide students with opportunities to hear a variety of points of view. They also provide limited space for all to articulate their ideas and engage in discussion with others. As an alternative, consider trying one-on-one pairs or small-group discussions. From those discussions, students can share interesting contrasts and similarities as well as questions on which they seek wider input from others.

Consider affinity-group discussions. Affinity groups allow students to share ideas with others who have similar backgrounds and experiences. Affinity groups might include students who identify as conservative or liberal, White or students of color, economically privileged or economically poor. One benefit of affinity groups is that students who often feel that others marginalize their experiences find an audience that understands their point of reference. They may also feel more comfortable sharing ideas without fear of being misunderstood. When ideas from affinity-group discussions are shared with the whole class, everyone benefits from hearing points of view that might not have been expressed in the larger group. These points of view can then become text for further reflection, again in affinity groups or in the whole class.

Set out the terrain for conflict. Often faculty understand the larger terrain (e.g., the social or political context) shaping any discussion before they ask students to talk. Students may not see that terrain. And not knowing that terrain may diminish the depth of their reflection or their sensitivity to others when talking. When faculty name and identify larger tensions and multiple framings of an issue before students engage in discussion, they prepare students to be more thoughtful and open-minded. In Chapter 14 Boesch's commitment to helping students see more than one way of understanding their service-learning experience is a concrete example of providing theoretical frameworks to understand experience.

Mentor and advise students. Not all education takes place in the class-room. Much learning also takes place in the context of mentoring and informal learning situations that are set apart from rules about required attendance and unconstrained by students' desire to get a good grade or fear of a bad one. In such situations, faculty and students can talk more freely with each other and be more open to challenge and change. While sheer limits on time prevent faculty from turning every potential difference or possible conflict into an opportunity for individual mentoring or independent and informal small-group learning, most faculty do routinely engage with students in this kind of context. In Chapter 15 Van Cleave describes an especially powerful example of this strategy to help a student examine beliefs about religion and sexual orientation and to shape this students' future openness to differing beliefs and experiences. In Chapter 13 Yep describes how her one-on-one interactions with a student helped frame his ability to be a better listener.

Model how to think, talk, and respond to conflict. When faculty frame productive conflict and respond appropriately to unproductive tensions, conflict, stereotypes, and unexamined opinions, they serve as useful models for students. What makes these opportunities even more educative is making the modeling component explicit. Faculty should explain why they are framing discussions in certain ways and not others. They should tell students, perhaps at a following class session, what they were thinking and why they responded the way they did to an instance of unproductive conflict. They should explain what they hope students gain from such a situation. Kohn (2004) calls this strategy *deep modeling* when educators explain what and why they are doing something alongside the actual doing.

Most of all, faculty can model conflict and negotiation as opportunities for transformation and growth. Working through conflict is a touchstone of *cultural humility* (Tervalon & Murray-García, 1998). Cultural humility blends knowledge, skills, and awareness of one's own and others' culture with ongoing reflection, self-assessment, and critique about power imbalances that exist between individuals and groups from different backgrounds. Cultural humility is a lifelong transformational process rather than an end point in understanding culture in connection to self and others. Martinuzzi (2007) wrote that

> when we approach situations from a perspective of humility, it opens us up to possibilities, as we choose open-mindedness and curiosity over protecting our point of view. We spend more time in that wonderful space of

the beginner's mind, willing to learn from what others have to offer. We move away from pushing into allowing, from insecure to secure, from seeking approval to seeking enlightenment. (para. 11)

Cultural humility has its place during discussions of inherently value-laden, controversial issues. These characteristics of cultural humility also describe the qualities of readiness for democratic participation described a century ago by Dewey (1916) and more recently by Colby, Beaumont, Ehrlich, and Corngold (2007): a commitment to understanding others, an openness to multiple points of view, a readiness to work across differences, and a desire to learn more. Faculty, like those in the chapters that follow, can then be role models of cultural humility and what might be called *democratic humility*, a similarly lifelong transformational process of understanding self and others in the context of political community.

References

Colby, A., Beaumont, E., Ehrlich, T., & Corngold, J. (2007). *Educating for democracy: Preparing undergraduates for responsible political engagement.* San Francisco, CA: Jossey-Bass.

Dewey, J. (1916). *Democracy and education.* New York, NY: Macmillan.

Dewey, J. (1938). *Experience and education.* New York, NY: Collier Books.

Ford, T. (Director). (2009). *A single man* [Motion picture]. USA: Sony Pictures.

Freire, P. (1970). *Pedagogy of the oppressed.* New York, NY: Continuum.

Kohn, A. (2004). Challenging students . . . and how to have more of them. *Phi Delta Kappan, 86*(3), 184–194.

Martinuzzi, B. (2007). *Humility: The most beautiful word in the English language.* http://www.mindtools.com/pages/article/newLDR_69.htm

Tervalon, M., & Murray-García, J. (1998). Cultural humility versus cultural competence: A critical distinction in defining physician training outcomes in multicultural education. *Journal of Health Care for the Poor and Underserved, 9*(2), 117–125.

Vygotsky, L. (1978). *Mind in society: The development of higher psychological processes.* Cambridge, MA: Harvard University Press.

13

WHY ARE YOU SO MAD?

Critical Multiculturalist Pedagogies and Mediating
Racial Conflicts in Community-Based Learning

Kathleen S. Yep

"Why do you always want to talk about race?
Can't we move beyond that?" (A White student
addressing students of color in the class)
"You need to hear this."
—Student of color addressing
White students in the class

A s the class discusses the community partner site in our service-learning course, I see a student grab her head in frustration and groan
loudly as another student speaks. Michael, a middle-class White student, has frequently expressed views about youth of color that differ radically
from the views of other White students and students of color in the class. I
can tell from across the room he has done it again.

Racial Divides in the Classroom

One challenge to teaching a community-based-learning course focused on
political engagement is addressing racial conflict in the classroom. I often
have to navigate between groups of students who have counter analyses
about the causes of poverty and racial discrimination. At times students
speak strongly toward each other or shut each other out based on different
life experiences with racism, White privilege, and poverty. According to
Peter McLaren (1997), critical multiculturalism interrogates difference in

relation to power and privilege rather than glossing it over under the rhetoric of inclusion and unity. While uncomfortable for the instructor and students alike, learning how to mediate various social locations and racial conflicts in the classroom is a stepping-stone for effectively engaging students with politics and political differences in the broader society (Torres, 1998).

In this community-based learning sociology class, I focused on developing students' understanding of patriarchy and the interlocking systems of oppression by forming a partnership with a high school at a local juvenile detention center. I organized the class around questions such as, What is patriarchy? What social functions does it serve? How does it relate to other axes of power? How do people challenge interlocking systems of oppression?

Based on scholarship by Featherstone and Ishibashi (2006) a series of class assignments invited students to analyze the democratic dilemmas of privilege in society, in their lives, and at the local juvenile detention center. To contextualize the community partnership, college students read about the racial and class politics of the prison industrial complex (Wilson Gilmore, 2007). The college class was composed of mostly White and East Asian students, while the high school class members primarily self-identified as African American and Latino. Using work by Mitchell (2008), the college students evaluated their sociological and cultural assets and examined similarities and differences between themselves and the high school students in an effort to address those gaps during their interactions.

Sociological Perspectives and Classroom Tensions

At the beginning of the semester, I emphasized understanding biological essentialism versus social constructs of gender (Kimmel, 2000). We discussed gender as more than just identity politics of women, but gender as a system that is circulated widely at the institutional level (Connell, 2005). Moreover, we explored the links among patriarchy, heteronormativity, and White privilege as intersecting ideological systems that have material consequences (Collins, 2000). Since patriarchy influences political life, I aimed to strengthen students' conceptual and practical understanding of how patriarchy and matrices of domination operate in society. In this way, students increased their political knowledge and skills by being able to identify and analyze how patriarchy and Whiteness act in concert with other systems of oppression.

However, these learning goals were not always readily achieved. To return to Michael, students individually expressed to me their frustration with his cheery but ill-informed comments about course content and social processes. A working-class Asian American student, Kelly, came to my office ostensibly to express her concerns with the community partnership.

What emerged in the conversation was her resentment toward Michael for making generalizations about working-class students of color. Kelly said she was "tired of teaching White people" and asked if I could play a more aggressive role in silencing Michael. Otherwise, she was considering dropping the class because she "just couldn't deal with another student like this again."

Then, a White student, Homer, hovered after class to talk with me. Homer came from a lower socioeconomic background than Michael's. Whereas Michael viewed the community partnership as providing a service to less-privileged individuals, Homer approached community-based learning as working beside the community partners toward the larger goal of social justice and the kind of wide-scale social change Butin (2010) discusses. Homer shared that he struggled in his conversations with Michael and felt more aligned with the students of color because of his previous experiences studying Whiteness and working in solidarity with students of color. Yet Homer felt unsure of what role he should take in the class since he did not want to be "another White guy talking all the time," as Messner (2000) has described. Consequently, Homer chose to stay silent but felt like he was going to explode after each class session.

Instructor Intervention

To address these class dynamics, I moved students into groups of three and provided discussion questions based on the readings. Each member of the group had a role as a note taker, facilitator, or presenter. The intent was to structure students' experiences in different roles as listeners, leaders, and speakers.

I also spoke with Michael after class to query his exposure to the concepts of White privilege and interlocking systems of oppression and found that he had little previous experience with readings such as those by Lipsitz (2006). With a color-blind framework, Michael viewed race as a matter of individual attitudes and beliefs rather than a web of "beliefs, . . . assumptions, policies, procedures, and laws . . . embedded in historic systems of oppression that sustain wealth, power, and privilege" (Featherstone & Ishibashi, 2006, p. 105). Moreover, Michael was unfamiliar with critical pedagogies as described by Freire (1998). Socialized to view education as an individual and competitive process, Michael tended to disregard the college and high school students and only directed comments to me rather than seeing the benefits of collaborating with his fellow students. This simple but significant discovery necessitated that I introduce him to methods of democratic learning through multiple types of discussion configurations. In addition, based on James's (M. James, personal communication, August 8, 2004) ideas of education for critical consciousness, I engaged the class in group consensus with general agreements regarding the classroom learning community protocols including assessing one's own views, making multiple attempts to see other views, balancing listening and talking, maintaining confidentiality, and refraining from insults.

Another instructional intervention was to roam among the students and listen to the small-group discussions. If needed, I redirected questions so that everyone participated. I also specifically asked if everyone was engaged and gently reminded the groups of the learning agreements. This created space for all students to pause and assess their role in the group process. Furthermore, the learning agreements provided a framework for students who felt silenced to speak up and to mindfully initiate asking questions or offering comments. In this way, Homer, Kelly, and Michael felt supported, yet also learned how to co-create a more equitable discussion in the small groups. Rather than impatiently waiting until the next speaker was finished to rush in with their own statement (neither listening to the previous speaker nor connecting their analysis) they now listened as a collective and relational act of dialogue and community building. This critical act of listening did not eclipse various viewpoints and social locations (Mathieson, 2004). Instead, students created mutual respect while recognizing the contradictions in their own multiple subjectivities and the differences in social locations in the group (Sasaki, 2002). By linking their ideas with others, they honed an essential tool for engaging with difference rather than eliding it.

Confrontations and Critical Teaching Moments

Although I took a proactive role in redirecting conversations, class anger at Michael escalated on the day he discussed his presentation of college information to the high school students. Michael was outraged that the high school students and the high school teacher did not pay attention to his presentation. In response, one classmate stated, "What do you expect if the high school students are struggling to stay alive?" Michael responded curtly, "I am just trying to help them." At this point, other students in the class no longer tried to hide their contempt for Michael. The verbal confrontations were direct and hostile. I stopped the class. I asked the students to pull out a piece of paper and write an open-ended question and put a symbol instead of their name on the paper. They folded their papers and placed them on a desk in the middle of the classroom. I shuffled the papers and then students randomly picked a paper and wrote their response to the question on the paper they selected. After five minutes, I asked students to close their response to the question they were working on with another open-ended question. Then they passed their paper to the person on their right, and each student wrote a response to the new question. Students retrieved their original paper and read the other students' responses to their first question. We closed the class with the students writing a final response to all the responses on their original paper.

My goal was to prevent the conflict from spiraling via personal attacks. My intention was to shift the class into more nonviolent forms of communication as conceptualized by Hanh (2003). In that heated moment, the college students needed constructive outlets to express their points of view, to be witnessed, to confront differing opinions in constructive ways, and to engage in dialogue. The writing supported everyone in the class and at the same time democratized who speaks and who listens in class. Learning how to confront the social context of difference and provide the space to reflect mindfully and collectively is an important skill for any form of political engagement in society, whether in electoral campaigns or in a community mobilization effort.

Moreover, I wanted to transform a personal statement into an analytical statement. The conflict emerged in part because the students focused only on the individual relationships, whether with Michael or the high school students. Rather than examining only individuals, students needed to analyze the interplay of institutions, ideologies, and individuals and in the context of interlocking social inequalities. For example, in a subsequent class meeting, Michael stated, "At the juvenile detention center, it's always the Black kids who are getting in trouble. They aren't interested in learning at all." As soon as Michael voiced this opinion, some students rolled their eyes while others muttered words of disgust. Several hands shot in the air as students readied themselves to confront Michael. Again I intervened and talked about the architecture of analytical inquiry. I wanted, on the one hand, to honor the right for everyone to speak, while, on the other, I sought to guide the class to broader critical analysis of how patriarchy, poverty, Whiteness, and heteronormativity intersect rather than simply target individual statements and opinions.

Influenced by Paulo Freire's (1970/2000) "problem-posing pedagogies," I shifted the focus toward naming a social contradiction, identifying the social causes to the contradiction, and coming up with solutions. I asked students to work in pairs and discuss a contradiction they observed at the juvenile detention center and then invited students to put their cogenerated contradictions on the board. Students wrote observations such as, "Teachers are disciplining only Black students even though all students are acting out" and "The high school students say sexist comments as we learn about Brown and Black empowerment." We mutually edited some of the statements to change them into observations rather than judgments. Then I asked the pairs to pick one observation from the board, write a why question based on the observable phenomenon, and relate it to the themes of the course. Students next wrote their research questions on the board: "Why are there higher rates of discipline for Black students than working-class White students?" and "Why is racial empowerment separated from feminism in the curriculum?" Finally, the pairs designed a research proposal based on their research question and possible explanations at the institutional, ideological, and individual level.

Critical Pedagogy and Long-Term Learning Outcomes

In the long term, I wanted to strengthen all the students' analytical skills by engaging a systematic analysis of power and privilege and placing the individual within a larger context (Kandaswamy, 2008; Kiang, 2003). In this case students learned not to dismiss individuals, including Michael or the high school students. Instead, they cultivated the critical political tool of exploring the institutional and ideological contexts for individual actions and ascertained how systems of oppression are mutually constitutive (Okazawa-Rey, 2008). Critical multiculturalist pedagogies helped students move away from either tolerating differences or dismissing others in a dehumanizing way. Through dialogue, students learned how to "work from . . . diverse situated knowledges" (McLaren, 1997, p. 295) and the asymmetrical relations of power. Consequently, no one fully relinquished her or his own agency and humanity in the midst of conflict by silently fuming or by bulldozing over others. Kelly learned to confront someone and an issue in a direct and constructive way rather than disengaging (Lorde, 1984). As a White ally, Homer understood his social responsibility and did not leave it to the students of color to address racism and White privilege (Howard, 2006). Michael eventually began to listen to and collaborate with others, using Homer as a role model. By learning a specific methodology for examining social inequalities, the college students are now better able to apply it to any social contradiction in society and craft constructive dialogues on volatile social issues.

If the objectives of community-based-learning courses are to teach democracy and political engagement, then there must be an understanding that both of these occur in the context of power, privilege, and the matrices of oppressions (Sleeter, 1996). Practicing democracy in a multiracial society is inextricably bound with navigating the complexities of social inequalities and privilege. As such, we must equip people with the practical and analytical tools to engage with conflict and various positions of privilege. Balancing an analysis of the interlocking systems of oppression with healthy dialogue is challenging yet crucial to antiracist pedagogies and to creating social equality (Omatsu, 2003; Shor, 1992). As such, in future community-based learning courses, I will emphasize how to process conflict to the same extent as reflecting on and analyzing social issues. I will provide explicit scaffolding for linking classroom dynamics to the larger political context, because racial formations, patriarchy, heteronormativity, and poverty are intersecting social processes that manifest themselves in the college classroom and in community partnerships. I will assist students with seeing that what they are learning in the course about creating dialogue is also a set of tools for creating democratic spaces in a multicultural society that does not minimize social contradictions but instead faces such issues directly.

References

Butin, D. W. (2010). *Service-learning in theory and practice: The future of community engagement in higher education.* New York, NY: Palgrave.

Collins, P. H. (2000). *Black feminist thought: Knowledge, consciousness, and the politics of empowerment* (2nd ed.). New York, NY: Routledge.

Connell, R. W. (2005). *Masculinities* (2nd ed.). Berkeley, CA: University of California Press.

Featherstone, E., & Ishibashi, J. (2006). Oreos and bananas: Conversations on whiteness. In V. Lea & J. Helfand (Eds.), *Identifying race and transforming whiteness in the classroom* (pp. 87–108). New York, NY: Peter Lang.

Freire, P. (1998). *Pedagogy of freedom: Ethics, democracy and civic courage* (P. Clarke, Trans.). New York, NY: Rowman & Littlefield.

Freire, P. (2000). *Pedagogy of the oppressed* (M. B. Ramos, Trans.). New York, NY: Continuum. (Original work published 1970)

Hanh, T. N. (2003). *Creating true peace: Ending violence in yourself, your family, your community, and the world.* New York, NY: The Free Press.

Howard, G. (2006). *We can't teach what we don't know: White teachers, multiracial schools* (2nd ed.). New York, NY: Teachers College Press.

Kandaswamy, P. (2008). Beyond colorblindness and multiculturalism: Rethinking anti-racist pedagogy in the university classroom. *Radical Teacher, 80,* 6–11.

Kiang, P. (2003). Pedagogies of PTSD: Circles of healing with refugees and veterans in Asian American studies. In L. Zhan (Ed.), *Asian Americans: Vulnerable populations, model interventions, and clarifying agendas* (pp. 197–222). Sudbury, MA: Jones and Bartlett.

Kimmel, M. (2000). *The gendered society.* New York, NY: Oxford University Press.

Lipsitz, G. (2006). *The possessive investment of whiteness* (2nd ed.). Philadelphia, PA: Temple University Press.

Lorde, A. (1984). *Sister outsider: Essays and speeches.* Berkeley, CA: The Crossing Press.

Mathieson, G. (2004). Reconceptualizing our classroom practice: Notes from an antiracist educator. In V. Lea & J. Helfand (Eds.), *Identifying race and transforming whiteness in the classroom* (pp. 235–256). New York, NY: Peter Lang.

McLaren, P. (1997). *Revolutionary multiculturalism: Pedagogies of dissent for the new millennium.* Boulder, CO: Westview Press.

Messner, M. (2000). White guy habitus in the classroom: Challenging the reproduction of privilege. *Men and Masculinities, 2,* 457–469.

Mitchell, T. D. (2008). Traditional vs. critical service-learning: Engaging the literature to differentiate two models. *Michigan Journal of Community Service Learning, 14*(2), 50–65.

Okazawa-Rey, M. (2008). Educating for critical practice. In E. Lee, D. Menkart, & M. Okazawa-Rey (Eds.), *Beyond heroes and holidays: A practical guide to K–12 anti-racist, multicultural education and staff development* (pp. 19–25). Washington, DC: Teaching for Change.

Omatsu, G. (2003). Freedom schooling: Reconceptualizing Asian American studies for our communities. *Amerasia Journal, 29*(2), 9–34.

Sasaki, B. (2002). Towards a pedagogy of coalition. In S. Sanchez and A. MacDonald (Eds.), *Twenty-first-century feminist classrooms: Pedagogies of identities and difference* (pp. 31–58). New York, NY: Palgrave MacMillan.

Shor, I. (1992). *Empowering education: Critical teaching for social change.* Chicago, IL: University of Chicago Press.

Sleeter, C. E. (1996). *Multicultural education as social activism.* Albany, NY: SUNY Press.

Torres, C. A. (1998). *Democracy, education, and multiculturalism: Dilemmas of citizenship in a global world.* New York: NY: Rowman & Littlefield.

Wilson Gilmore, R. (2007). *Golden gulag: Prisons, surplus, crisis, and opposition in globalizing California.* Berkeley, CA: University of California Press.

14

WORKING WITH HIGH SCHOOL DROPOUTS

Service-Learning Illustrations of Power and Privilege

Becky Boesch

Having used service-learning since 1994 ranging from tutoring English as a Second Language students in public schools to removing invasive species from national lands, I was prepared for all types of issues in college learning communities, or so I thought, until an intellectual impasse surfaced between the students and myself. The senior capstone service-learning course was designed to develop civic awareness as a culmination of a student's experience in college. Intentionally small at 15 students to optimize learning, Alternative School Youth: Educational Mentoring for High School Dropouts incorporated critical theory as a framework for examining how power and oppression are manifested among different societal groups. Critical theory assumes that social inequities exist and are perpetuated in cultural and institutional systems and that "one of the major tasks of a critical analysis is to uncover and expose these power relationships wherein the domination of one group's interests results in the oppression of other groups" (Merriam & Caffarella, 1999, p. 347).

The capstone course seemed the perfect avenue for raising student social awareness regarding educational achievement gaps. Our community partner was an agency with programs for individuals who dropped out of high school. Students in this service-learning course would tutor and mentor these individuals to obtain their General Education Degree (GED). I hoped the service-learning experience would help students understand how our educational system privileges some students and disadvantages others. I hoped they would leave the course as vehicles for social change in educational reform.

Besides tutoring others, the college students kept mentoring journals to analyze how social, familial, educational, and financial forces have affected and were still having an impact on individual efforts to earn a GED. For context, students read a mentoring book (Zachary, 2000); a manuscript of case studies on at-risk students (Aronson, 2001); and *Privilege, Power, and Difference* (Johnson, 1997), which examines how power and privilege are manifested in areas of gender, race, and social class. As Johnson states, "[There is] a yawning divide in levels of income, wealth, dignity, safety, health, and quality of life. . . . It weaves the insidious and corroding effects of oppression into the daily lives of tens of millions of women, men and children" (p. 9).

I had used part of this text previously in freshman courses and had found it worked well in helping students recognize how they either benefited from or were victims of systemic oppression. While freshmen (particularly those who were privileged) sometimes initially struggled with recognizing or acknowledging the issues of privilege and oppression, throughout the duration of the course the majority of freshmen usually came to understand these concepts on a personal and societal level. In this case, I assumed that seniors with more sophisticated academic development would have no problem seeing the manifestations of power and privilege at their service-learning site. I could not have been more wrong.

Differing Perspectives on Power and Privilege

The class began with an innocence and eagerness for service-learning, but by the second week, having read the first two chapters of Johnson (1997), students appeared irritated with Johnson's ideas. I attributed it to the initial discomfort most students feel when they acknowledge being a recipient of privilege and power simply because of the color of their skin, gender, or social class. At the same time it is difficult to acknowledge that others suffer from a lack of privilege based on these same characteristics and that your own actions may perpetuate this inequity knowingly or unknowingly.

To visually highlight concepts of privilege, we viewed Jane Elliott's 1996 film *Blue-Eyed*, which illustrates social constructions of power and oppression. The students erupted with passionate disbelief that systems of power and privilege exist. Others acknowledged that perhaps they existed but not to the degree that either Johnson (1997) or Elliot (1996) maintained. Student frustration encompassed their service-learning site. The class consensus was that if someone dropped out of high school, it was because he or she chose to as an individual and not because the system did not allow one to succeed. Students asserted that if you couldn't succeed in American society, then you didn't try hard enough.

I was stupefied. Johnson (1997) writes that "the social world consists of a lot more than individuals. We are always participating in something larger than ourselves—what sociologists call social systems—and systems are more than collections of people" (p. 85). Yet in students' minds, American democratic values of individualism and meritocracy (hard work reaps equal rewards) negated any oppressive social forces. Indeed, students blamed victims for not overcoming their circumstances (Ryan, 1971). My exploration of power and privilege had seriously backfired. Students seemed further entrenched in their thinking.

I consulted a couple of trusted colleagues and came to realize that my fatal error had been false assumptions regarding students' cognitive development. I assumed that because they were college seniors, according to Perry (1970) and Kitchener and King's (1981) Reflective Judgment Model, the majority of students would be capable of relativistic thinking where diversity of opinion, values, and judgment derived from coherent sources, evidence, logic, systems, and patterns allowing for analysis and comparison. Instead, student perspectives were dualistic; they blamed the individual or society but were incapable of understanding the interactive interdependence of the person and social systems. A few students could identify and legitimate multiple causes for educational achievement gaps but in doing so remained relatively neutral in their stance on causation.

Pedagogical Redirection

As the instructor, I bore responsibility for leading them toward a new kind of critical consciousness (Freire, 1970/1993). I needed to show them the process for critically deconstructing their own perspectives and assumptions. I had to teach them how to engage in reflective judgment processes as a classroom community. I tried to coax, cajole, and convince students to reexamine their perspectives on power and privilege through mini lectures and class discussions on the readings, but the real pedagogical moment for learning redirection came in the midst of student complaints about their mentees. The students were required to mentor 4 hours per week and then reflect on their experiences in journal writings and ethnographies, but the mentees began missing their sessions. Instantly students resorted to individual blaming. "They aren't taking their education seriously." "They don't care about my time, why should I care about their education if they don't." "I think they are just lazy."

To counter these perspectives, we drew from readings on teaching and learning processes (Palmer, 1998) and outlined on the board possible personal, community, and societal factors that contribute to educational failure. Then I encouraged the students to find out why these individuals were missing their sessions. One girl missed frequently because her mother, a single mom, worked irregular hours and the girl needed to stay home and watch her younger sisters and brothers because child care was not affordable. A young man was experiencing pressure to join a gang, so he stayed home to avoid possible confrontations with gang members. A girl from an abusive home had moved in with her boyfriend and now was pregnant. Another girl had entered her mother into a drug treatment program and had to miss several classes to help oversee the process. Still another mentee had not missed a single session but was simply unwilling to take the GED test for fear of failing.

As students got to know their mentees better, they began to realize that mentees' struggles in completing their GED could not be attributed merely to individual desire or motivation. Instead, their mentees were caught in social webs and systems that severely weakened the power of the individual to orchestrate change. As we debriefed their mentor sessions, students increasingly referred to the reading concepts and articulated how systems of power and privilege were thwarting their mentees' lives. While a few students remained steadfast in their views that everyone could succeed if they really wanted to, other students began to challenge these ideas and offered new insights on inequities in school and in social, economic, and political systems. They participated in individual and classroom reflective judgment and thinking.

In hindsight, even after two decades of teaching, I now better understand how students need cognitive scaffolding for building and expanding their conceptual frameworks and perspectives. But the intellectual realm is not enough to truly facilitate student critical thinking; testing and applying ideas in the community is essential. Service-learning is an incredible vehicle for creating democratic communities because it forces us and our students to examine dilemmas of power, privilege, and disadvantage in the lives of real people. Similarly, if I am truly committed as an educator to raising students' social awareness about the inequities caused by race, gender, and class, then I must be pedagogically prepared to encounter intellectual and emotional resistance from students in assisting them to become agents of community change.

References

Aronson, R. (2001). *At-risk students defy the odds: Overcoming barriers to educational success.* Lanham, MD: Scarecrow Press.

Elliott, J. (1996). *Blue-Eyed* (Video). Munchen, Germany: DENKmal-Film, GMBH.

Freire, P. (1993). *Pedagogy of the oppressed* (M. B. Ramos, Trans.). New York, NY: Continuum. (Original work published 1970)

Johnson, A. (1997). *Privilege, power, and difference.* Boston, MA: McGraw-Hill.

Kitchener, K. S., & King, P. M. (1981). Reflective judgment: Concepts of justification and their relationship to age and education. *Journal of Applied Developmental Psychology, 2,* 89–116.

Merriam, S., & Caffarella, R. (1999). *Learning in adulthood: A comprehensive guide* (2nd ed.) San Francisco, CA: Jossey-Bass.

Palmer, P. (1998). *The courage to teach.* San Francisco, CA: Jossey-Bass.

Perry, W. G. (1970). *Form of intellectual and ethical development in the college years.* Austin, TX: Holt, Rinehart and Winston.

Ryan, W. (1971). *Blaming the victim.* Pantheon Books Scale of Intellectual Development. New York, NY: Pantheon Books.

Zachary, L. J. (2000). *The mentor's guide: Facilitating effective learning relationships.* San Francisco, CA: Jossey-Bass.

15

DEMOCRATIC LESSONS IN FAITH, SERVICE, AND SEXUALITY

Thomas J. Van Cleave

While working for a large faith-based organization situated at a public higher education institution, I collaborated with the college to develop short-term service-learning opportunities for students over winter and spring breaks. We provided nearly 400 students with opportunities in 19 locations across the nation and globe including sites focused on health care, natural disaster reconstruction, international prison conditions, rural and urban poverty, substance abuse, and the foster care system.

Organizationally, we were democratically separate entities—one was the church and one was the state. But we coexisted harmoniously in our mutual goals for improving community and human life through service-learning. Our students, however, sometimes struggled with crossing these public and private bridges between serving others and "saving" others. As a service-learning facilitator at some of the sites, I witnessed firsthand how some students involved themselves in charity work as a means of trying to convert others as a requirement of their faith, while other students' views were dismantled by the service-learning experience when their beliefs clashed with those of other individuals and with alternative lifestyles. In group discussions and journals, students wrestled with what it means to individuate themselves from their parents, families, home churches, communities, and even their college peers, which was evidence they were pursuing self-authorship in trying to reconcile the relationship between individual and community (Chickering & Reisser, 1993).

The clashing of ideals, beliefs, and perspectives is not new to anyone in education or service-learning. Indeed, it is an opportunity for growth and development. But knowing how to negotiate discussions and learning across strict religious perspectives can challenge the service-learning instructor and student alike. In fact, that was the case with Daniel.

Daniel had requested a meeting to discuss one of the spring break service-learning opportunities. Armed with his Bible, a sheet of notebook paper covered with notes, and a concerned look on his face, Daniel wasted no time wanting to know why our faith-based organization would form a partnership with an organization that served people infected with HIV/AIDS. According to Daniel, because homosexuality was "obviously" contrary to scripture, it was against God's will that as members of a Christian organization we would support what he called "an abomination." Daniel believed HIV/AIDS was God's curse on the homosexual community for its rebellion. His pastor said so, his parents said so, and his culture said so. By working with this community agency, we were conspiring with the college in violating Daniel's Christianity through secularism.

The university was located in a very conservative area in the Midwest. Daniel was born and raised less than 10 miles from the campus. Daniel had never been friends with someone from a different faith background but claimed he knew a handful of practicing Catholics, a few ethnic minorities, but no gays. He felt victimized as a Christian by the liberal perspectives in his classrooms and now felt further undermined by an organization that was supposed to support his beliefs. How could we provide service to those destined for hell?

Ways of Faith and Knowing

Daniel was a part of the sexual, cultural, religious, and racial majority. Alternative doctrine, ways of life, and ways of being were far from Daniel's lived experiences. Daniel had yet to be exposed to what Zaytoun (2005) describes as "the complexities in points of view that emerge from experiencing multiplicity" (p. 13). Daniel's way of believing and knowing came from "truth" that flowed directly from experts who are qualified to know and explain truth to amateurs who are qualified only to receive truth (Baxter Magolda, 1992;

Belenky, Clinchy, Goldberger, & Tarule, 1986). Daniel's truth was that we were contradicting ourselves as a Christian organization, and as a common community of believers we should support service-learning sites consistent with our faith.

Knowing and truth for Daniel had one right answer and one way of being. While I felt biblically competent to engage with him in a scripture debate, I proposed instead that Daniel, myself, and a few other students interested in the topic meet regularly to discuss the subject. Together we would form a unique learning community described by Palmer (2007):

> [To] understand the subject in the community of truth, we enter into complex patterns of communication—sharing observations and interpretations, correcting and complementing each other, torn by conflict in this moment and joined by consensus in the next. The community of truth, far from being linear and static and hierarchical, is circular, interactive and dynamic. (p. 106)

This was the first time Daniel had ever been a part of a community of shared power and differing perspectives. His previous learning and religious faith had been defined by hierarchy. Now he collaboratively participated in creating guidelines for group discussion and collectively strategized about how to honor controversy with civility (Astin & Astin, 1996). We met for 6 weeks with students discussing definitions and views on scripture, service-learning, and sexuality. Each member took turns initiating and facilitating the discussion. Probably the most powerful moments were student descriptions of interacting with family or friends who are gay and how they grappled with their own spirituality in light of these disclosures. And as a community, the group came to a consensus that providing service-learning for those with differing beliefs and ways of living was completely appropriate for the Christian organization. Even Daniel eventually shared this perspective.

We all form opinions and judge right from wrong by what Kuhn (1970) calls *paradigms*. These paradigms are influenced by early caregivers, like parents, and serve as collective "beliefs, values, techniques . . . shared by the members of a given community" (p. 175). Daniel was moving out of the hierarchy of truth into a contextual community of truth (Palmer, 2007).

For Daniel, college was the first experience of what Taylor (2008) refers to as *dissonance*, opinions and ways of being contrary to one's own. Dissonance, however, is not an entirely negative phenomenon. It can serve as a catalyst for development, but it takes great courage. As Robertson (1996) notes, it is not easy for people to think or feel in a way that is contrary to everything they know and with which they are comfortable. As Chickering and Reisser (1993) explain, students may feel "anxiety or specific fear of discovery and punishment from parents, church, or educational institutions when their way of thinking shifts away from culturally programmed responses" (p. 51).

Certainly issues of dissonance are often faced by students and faculty in service-learning experiences, as paradigmatic ways of thinking and operating are challenged by individuals and communities with differing perspectives. Perhaps that is the greatest democratic lesson we can offer our students through service-learning: feeling comfortable in the dissonance of difference.

As for Daniel, he selected a service-learning experience in Costa Rica working with orphans. But he now has a diverse group of friends, including some of different religious backgrounds, race/ethnicity, and even sexual orientation. A few months ago Daniel sent me an e-mail with a quote we regularly read in our discussion group. Henri Nouwen (1989) said, "Jesus has a different vision of maturity: It is the willingness to be led where you would rather not go" (p. 83). And Daniel added "and engaging with community that you didn't know you could."

References

Astin, A., & Astin, H. (1996). *A social change model of leadership development.* Los Angeles, CA: Higher Education Research Institute.

Baxter Magolda, M. (1992). *Knowing and reasoning in college: Gender-related patterns in students' intellectual development.* San Francisco, CA: Jossey-Bass.

Belenky, M. F., Clinchy, B. M., Goldberger, N. R., & Tarule, J. M. (1986). *Women's ways of knowing: The development of self, voice, and mind.* New York, NY: Basic Books.

Chickering, A. W., & Reisser, L. (1993). *Education and identity.* San Francisco, CA: Jossey-Bass.

Kuhn, T. S. (1970). *The structure of scientific revolutions.* Chicago, IL: University of Chicago Press.

Nouwen, H. J. M. (1989). *In the name of Jesus: Reflections on Christian leadership.* Atlanta, GA: Crossroad.

Palmer, P. J. (2007). *The courage to teach: Exploring the inner landscape of a teacher's life.* San Francisco, CA: Jossey-Bass.

Robertson, D. N. (1996). Facilitating transformative learning: Attending to the dynamics of the educational helping relationship. *Adult Education Quarterly,* *47*(1), 41–53.

Taylor, K. B. (2008). Mapping the intricacies of young adults' developmental journey from socially prescribed to internally defined identities, relationships and beliefs. *Journal of College Student Development, 49*(3), 215–234.

Zaytoun, K. D. (2005). Identity and learning: The inextricable link. *About Campus, 9*(6), 8–15.

PART FIVE

ACADEMIC DISCIPLINES AS DIMENSIONS OF DEMOCRACY

16

DISCIPLINARY KNOWLEDGE, SERVICE-LEARNING, AND CITIZENSHIP

David M. Donahue

With heightened emphasis on accountability in education from preschool through graduate school and the accompanying tests that hold instructors and students accountable to those standards, it is easy to see how learning could be confused with knowing discrete, unconnected facts, and to forget that learning is ultimately about understanding, or, in other words, about being able to use knowledge flexibly in new situations and contexts. For over a century U.S. scholars of education, starting with John Dewey (1904), have reminded us that learning is about more than meeting narrowly defined conceptions of knowing. It is, among other things, about the goals of preparing students for critical thinking, imaginative problem solving, and participation in democratic life. These goals do not need to stand apart from courses in the disciplines making up a liberal arts education. The disciplines that define higher education can and should also be the contexts for these important kinds of learning.

This chapter describes how, in addition to having value in and of themselves, the various disciplines in higher education play a role in preparing students for the knowledge, skills, and dispositions required by civic and political life. It explains how the disciplines are venues for such preparation when faculty make thoughtful intentional decisions about the service-learning curriculum. It includes strategies that can be embedded in service-learning as part of subject matter courses that prepare students for life in democracy. This chapter also frames the vignettes in the following chapters by Christopher Brooks, Corey Cook, Sandra Sgoutas-Emch, and Kathleen Yep. Each author illustrates the connection between an academic discipline—computer science, political science, psychology, and Asian American studies—and learning about political life through service-learning.

Disciplinary Teaching and Worthwhile Learning

David Perkins (2009) describes how teaching complicated subject matter often becomes relegated to breaking down complex tasks into components that are learned separately and later—often much later—put together for use in the real world. He also describes how students learn about something rather than learn to do that same thing. He describes these twin phenomena as *elementitis* and *aboutitis*. Perkins encourages teachers to instead think about "making learning whole." Part of making learning whole is to ground any definition of understanding in the academic disciplines in performance. In other words, remembering information for a test is not a demonstration of understanding. Using information in new and authentic tasks is, however, a marker of understanding.

Several decades earlier, Joseph Schwab (1969) reminded educators that curriculum in the disciplines should be concerned with choice and action, not merely the theoretical; it should lead to defensible decisions and warranted conclusions. For Schwab, the academic disciplines are venues for learning how to solve problems. In that sense, curriculum in the disciplines is practical.

John Dewey (1904) noted this practical aspect of curriculum even earlier. While disciplinary knowledge has value in and of itself, that intrinsic value is of most concern to people conducting research in the disciplines. For those educating others, disciplinary knowledge has another value in contributing to experience that leads to further growth across domains from the intellectual to the personal, social, and civic. As college and university faculty, it is easy to conflate our roles as researchers and educators when we teach our students. Focusing on the role of an educator, however, Dewey wrote, "Hence, what concerns him, as a teacher, is the ways in which that subject may become a part of experience. . . . He is concerned not with the subject matter as such, but with the subject matter as a related factor in the total and growing experience" (pp. 285–286).

Service-learning provides a valuable opportunity for educators and students to reconceptualize subject matter knowledge according to Dewey's (1904) recommendation. Service-learning promotes the wholeness of learning and the performance definition of understanding described by Perkins (2009). Through service-learning, students go beyond elementitis and aboutitis to engage in tasks that require knowledge in and across the disciplines. This knowledge is not discrete but related to addressing real situations such as figuring out why technological resources are unequally distributed in a community or how to educate voters on ballot propositions. These tasks promote not only cognitive growth, but when scaffolded appropriately also nurture personal, social, and civic development. In reflecting on the digital divide, as Brooks does in Chapter 17, students can challenge their own assumptions about who uses technology, and they can work collectively to make technological resources more accessible and consider how long-term solutions require changes effected through democratic politics.

Service-learning also promotes the practical described by Schwab (1969). As students engage in action and thinking that do not necessarily follow the outlines of a textbook but follow the patterns of real problems in the world, they develop a deeper understanding of the practical or the relatedness of ideas within a discipline and across disciplines and how those ideas have use for guiding action in the world outside the classroom. Disciplinary knowledge becomes part of Dewey's (1904) "growing experience" across many dimensions of intellectual and social life.

Critical Thinking and the Disciplines

In addition to developing students' knowledge of subject-specific content, college and university courses are also sites for developing students' more general critical thinking. The National Council for Excellence in Critical Thinking (1987) defines critical thinking as

> the intellectually disciplined process of actively and skillfully conceptualizing, applying, analyzing, synthesizing, and/or evaluating information gathered from, or generated by, observation, experience, reflection, reasoning, or communication, as a guide to belief and action. (para. 3)

As the definition makes clear, critical thinking is a set of skills and a disposition to use those skills in all aspects of thinking and decision making. The definition continues,

It is based on universal intellectual values that transcend subject matter divisions: clarity, accuracy, precision, consistency, relevance, sound evidence, good reasons, depth, breadth, and fairness. (para. 3)

Although the skills and habits of critical thinking transcend the disciplines, teaching and learning in the individual disciplines that constitute a liberal arts education are not irrelevant to critical thinking. While some institutions offer stand-alone courses on critical thinking, most do not because such stand-alone courses represent a limited conception of critical thinking absent the content of critical thinking. Students must learn to think critically about something and that something or subject matter content is at the heart of disciplinary teaching and learning. All colleges and universities claim their graduates gain skill in critical thinking. If that is the case, then faculty in the various disciplines are responsible for teaching such skills and dispositions.

In the vignettes in the following chapters in this section, teachers and students engage in numerous aspects of critical thinking. They raise questions. They develop plans for answering those questions including plans to collect and analyze data. They build knowledge using open minds and incorporating multiple perspectives. They reconsider their own assumptions and prior beliefs. The teachers and students are able to think about what they should do when they are not told what to do in detail in a textbook or lecture. They are motivated to engage in such thinking and action.

Service-learning can play a key role in creating opportunities for critical thinking, for example, in Corey Cook's political science class in Chapter 18. The project in that class put students in situations where they could not help but raise questions that had no easy answers, where they were motivated to engage in grappling with those thorny questions, and where they had access to multiple perspectives through community members and provocative texts that challenge their own assumptions. In other words, critical thinking was required and supported. The service-learning projects in the following chapters not only promote critical thinking, they help connect that thinking to democratic life (Cress, 2004). The projects raise dilemmas these skilled instructors make explicit and visible for students' consideration and as texts for their learning. Because these dilemmas have no single right answer and are located in the practical as described by Schwab (1969), they promote critical thinking skills such as weighing and sorting evidence, separating facts and opinion, and making sense of multiple and sometimes conflicting perspectives. The ability to ask good questions or the habit of challenging one's assumptions, for example, become skills and dispositions that serve political thinking and decision making, not only discipline-based scholarship.

Critical Consciousness and the Disciplines

Just as service-learning in the disciplines can promote critical thinking, it can also nurture critical consciousness, a concept related to critical thinking with implications for working toward a more equitable and just society (Cress, 2004). In *Pedagogy of the Oppressed*, Paulo Freire (1970) introduced the concept of *conscientization*, or critical consciousness. Critical consciousness recognizes oppression, external and internal, and works to undo oppression by liberating the oppressed and their oppressors from dehumanization. Education plays a key role in undoing oppression by posing problems about the individual's relations to the rest of the world. In this way, education is about a process of becoming (in this case becoming liberated from oppression) rather than a process of acquiring (a body of disconnected knowledge).

In Kathleen Yep's teaching case at the end of this section, students begin to develop critical consciousness through service-learning and through critical thinking about theoretical constructs that are key to the disciplines of sociology and ethnic studies. They do so by asking questions about their relationship to others around them and to phenomena that characterize worlds of inequality and injustice. The knowledge they build then is about becoming agents of change rather than having yet more privilege as a result of their experience. Service-learning plays a key role in students' growth. Service experiences put students in contexts where they observe or experience oppression and privilege. Using the critical thinking lens of Asian American Studies, Yep makes those observations and experiences the texts for reflection. This reflection leads students to develop habits of mind that make concepts such as oppression and privilege part of how they understand being in the world, not merely concepts that explain abstract phenomena unrelated to their own life.

The Political Dimension of Disciplinary Knowledge

Students are likely to see some academic disciplines as more political than others. While most students would consider political science as the most political of disciplines and computer science class as the least political, in fact all disciplines have a political dimension or connection. And all disciplines, including—ironically—political science, can be taught without any reference to current political issues. The question then is not, Which disciplines are political or lend themselves to thinking about democratic life? but How can the connections among disciplines ranging from psychology to ethnic studies, service-learning, and democratic life be made explicit for students?

While computer science faculty, as Brooks reports in Chapter 17, may face more initial resistance from students to addressing political issues, most faculty will find that students are not used to thinking about the political dimension of disciplinary course work and service-learning. Service-learning projects, however, can help students see that knowledge in the disciplines can be useful as part of democratic life. Disciplinary knowledge can inform political decision making. For instance, knowledge of computer science is important to understanding issues from net neutrality to electronic voting. While knowledge of political science might seem to have obvious applications to almost every political decision, knowledge of other disciplines can inform decision making on specific issues. When disciplinary course work and service-learning become grounds for fostering critical thinking and critical consciousness, then the disciplines foster habits of mind that serve students well as participants in democratic life. The key to helping them make such connections is to state them explicitly.

Strategies to Connect Disciplinary Knowledge to Service-Learning and Citizenship

With little extra effort, faculty can help students use the knowledge, skills, and dispositions of their discipline not only to deepen service-learning experiences but to further students' preparation for democratic life (Cress, Kerrigan, & Reitenauer, 2003). In most cases, these efforts require only being more explicit about what most instructors are probably already doing. All the following suggestions are interrelated.

Include a course objective connecting course content and political issues or processes. While most faculty want students to make connections between course content and democratic decision making, they may not make these priorities for student-learning. They may not even make them explicit to students, leaving these goals implicit and therefore invisible to some or seemingly unimportant to others. Service-learning projects have the most impact on learning when faculty develop a few explicit understanding goals. These goals help focus instruction and student learning. Less is more. Two or three goals are better than seven or eight. If one of these goals is to connect content knowledge to service and political participation and decision making, instructors can hold themselves and students accountable. Making these goals explicit to community partners also helps them support students in meeting the project's objectives. Making the goals explicit to students frames their learning throughout the semester. Making the goals explicit to yourself as the instructor reminds you why you are doing this work, something that is possible to forget in managing the logistics of service-learning.

Use ongoing reflection to promote connections between content and political life. Setting a goal is the first step. The next is to provide opportunities for students to engage in thinking that helps them achieve the goal. Toward that end, instructors should use reflection on service as an opportunity to prompt students to make connections between disciplinary content and political life. As Cook's teaching case in Chapter 18 illustrates, questions can encourage students to connect knowledge from the discipline to informed political decisions. They can prompt students to use habits of mind like critical thinking to reach logical, well-informed conclusions that honor multiple perspectives. They can spark the critical consciousness that leads to political action toward equity and justice.

Assess students' ability to connect disciplinary knowledge and political life. Assessment reminds students and faculty about what knowledge counts. Assessment also yields information to students about areas of growth and possibilities for future growth. Finally, assessment provides information to faculty on the success of course design and implementation. While midterm and final exams are obvious examples of assessment, faculty should also consider forms of ongoing assessment. These can be simple and quick. After a reflective conversation, students can spend the last minute of class writing the big idea they take away from the conversation on a 3-inch-by-5-inch card. The small size of the card forces them to be succinct and ensures that faculty are not overwhelmed with data. At the same time, such assessment gives instructors a valuable snapshot of students' thinking. Other examples of simple assessment include 3-minute writing assignments at the beginning of class reflecting on the class discussion in the previous session, one-sentence summaries of quick student pairs conversations, and "exit tickets" that students write at the end of class about one question they still have about connecting disciplinary content to political issues and processes. When faculty use strategies like these to promote reflection on students' experiences and make connections between the subject they teach and democratic life, students are more likely to understand, practice, and value such connections themselves.

References

Cress, C. M. (2004). Critical thinking development in service-learning activities: pedagogical implications for critical being and action. *Inquiry; Critical Thinking Across the Disciplines, 23,* 87–93.

Cress, C. M., Kerrigan, S., & Reitenauer, V. (Fall, 2003). Making community-based learning meaningful: Faculty efforts to increase student civic engagement skills. *Transformations: The Journal of Inclusive Scholarship and Pedagogy, xiv*(2), 87–100.

Dewey, J. (1904). *School and society.* Chicago, IL: University of Chicago Press.

Dewey, J. (1988). The child and the curriculum. In J. Boydston (Ed.), *John Dewey: The middle works, 1899–1924* (Vol. 2, pp. 273–291). Carbondale, IL: Southern Illinois University Press.

Freire, P. (1970). *Pedagogy of the oppressed* (M. B. Ramos, Trans.). New York, NY: Continuum.

National Council for Excellence in Critical Thinking. (1987). *Critical thinking as defined by the National Council for Excellence in Critical Thinking.* Retrieved from http://www.criticalthinking.org/aboutCT/define_critical_thinking.cfm

Perkins, D. (2009). *Making learning whole.* San Francisco, CA: Jossey-Bass.

Schwab, J. (1969). The practical: A language for curriculum. *School Review, 78*(1), 1–23.

17

WHY SHOULD I CARE?

Introducing Service-Learning and Political Engagement to Computer Science Students

Christopher Brooks

Since 2004 I have been teaching Computers and Society, an upper-division computer science course that examines the broader social impact of computing technology. Topics include information privacy, professional ethics, copyright, and file sharing, among others. The class also discusses the digital divide: unequal access to computers, the Internet, and effective training between different ages, economic classes, genders, and ethnic groups. Students are then expected as the service-learning requirement to work every week with a local organization such as a drop-in computer lab or an after-school program to try to help bridge the digital divide. Students maintain computer labs, set up and install software, teach classes, and tutor clients. By doing so, they see the impact that access to technology can have on the organization's clients, and they also get firsthand experience with the sorts of bureaucratic, financial, and technological challenges these organizations face.

Most local community organizations are severely understaffed and underfunded, which leads us to reflect in class on why our service is needed in the first place. Typically, this experience is very transformative for students; working with a population they do not normally encounter and seeing how access to and knowledge about information technology can change a person's life often causes our students to see their future as developers of that technology in a new light. However, solely providing direct service leaves students missing a fundamental piece of this problem: Why is it that this digital divide exists, and why are organizations working to bridge this digital divide so strapped for resources?

Computer Science and Political Engagement

I decided to integrate political engagement into Computers and Society to give the class an opportunity to address the dilemmas surrounding digital divides, specifically, why they exist. I was quite nervous about this addition. I had to make a sales pitch to students about the inclusion of service-learning as many of them were not interested in broader civic engagement, and, according to them, they majored in computer science precisely because they were more interested in computers, programming, and problem solving than in learning about social inequity. And while the notion of service had at least a mostly positive connotation, political engagement, on the other hand, was viewed quite negatively by my students.

Therefore, I chose to focus not on electoral politics, which seemed to be at the root of my students' cynicism, but on politics as a means of allocating resources. This let the class tackle head-on the question that their service was raising: Why is it that in one of the wealthiest cities on Earth, in the heart of the technology industry, there are people without access to computers or the knowledge of how to use them? Why do the organizations working to address this not have the resources they need?

Service Project Strategies

I began by inviting a representative from the San Francisco Department of Technology and Information Services (DTIS) to speak to our class. She described San Francisco's efforts to bridge the digital divide. We found out that much of the current efforts involved direct outreach to citizens, and there was not much support or funding for community organizations. In fact, there was not even a clear picture of which organizations provided training or access.

Based on this information, the class determined there was need for a tool that would help DTIS and the users of their computer labs to better understand what services were available, where they were located, and what areas and populations of the city were not being served. The class decided to develop a Web-based tool called SF TechCenter that would include a searchable database of drop-in labs, including neighborhood, lab resources, languages spoken, classes offered, and hours of operation. It also included a Google Maps–based tool that allowed clients and government employees to see where the city services were located.

The project gave students experience working in groups, using modern tools to share code, developing databases and Web-based applications, and assisting a real client on a project with changing, sometimes underspecified, outcomes. Several students wound up using this project as a showcase in their job search.

It also served to highlight the relationship between political engagement and the discipline of computer science in a way that was completely separate from electoral politics. Students came to understand how staff in a large governmental office work to address social equity dilemmas and the complexity and difficulty of even understanding the parameters of the problem much less articulating a solution. Most important, they developed an increased sense of agency and belief that they could influence the world around them utilizing their academic and career skills.

Incorporating service-learning and political engagement into a computer science course has been challenging but well worth it. It provided students with a new perspective on their discipline and the chance to connect their narrowly focused course material to a larger, more holistic view of how politics influences and is influenced by their field. Integrating these disparate topics successfully required instructional care and attention in helping students discover the connections between these topics. If the service-learning, political engagement, or computer science components had been merely tacked on, the whole learning experience probably would have failed. Carefully interconnecting the three allowed me to address students' concerns about the necessity of service and political engagement and bring a fresh, relevant dimension to issues of social justice in technology.

18

POLITICAL SCIENCE STUDENTS AND THE DISENGAGED POLIS

Civic Education and Its Discontents

Corey Cook

I have long been an avid proponent of service-learning as a pedagogical tool. But service-learning alone does not rectify the voter participation gap (Kirlin, 2002). Accordingly, I designed a project to employ service-learning methodologies to promote political engagement through a student-led civic education project embedded in an introductory course on American politics. The goal of the project was to have students prepare video voter guides to be shown on campus and posted on the Internet to increase the amount of information available to voters on state and local propositions. I hoped my students would become more informed about the issues, develop civic skills, and provide a worthwhile service to the university community.

I began the semester by giving students a broad outline of the project and sorted them randomly into groups to research and write scripts providing nonpartisan and empirically verifiable information about each ballot proposition. At the same time, students began reading Peter Levine's (2007) *The Future of Democracy: Developing the Next Generation of American Citizens.* Levine asserts that young people continue to be largely disengaged from political processes and lack basic political literacy. He identifies civic education as a public good and advocates for a series of programs for civic renewal. This engagement with the academic literature facilitated student discussion about the project. Students tended to agree with Levine's central thesis and, consequentially, embraced the service project as a means for educating voters about the issues and encouraging them to participate in the election.

Interestingly, students offered varying justifications for promoting civic education and revealed differing motives for the class project. The largest group of students articulated an argument based on equity: that unequal access to valid political information generates inequality in rates of participation that undermines the equality of voice inherent in fully democratic elections. These students embraced what I would loosely call a social justice conception of civic literacy and quickly turned the discussion from the underrepresentation of youth in the electorate to inequalities in turnout based on education, income, and home ownership.

A second group maintained that consent is only truly conferred in elections marked by high participation and informed knowledge about the ballot. These students seemed concerned primarily with the legitimacy of electoral outcomes. One student summed up this sentiment by questioning whether an election can be considered valid if a segment of the electorate bases its votes on anything short of full information about the likely consequences of that vote. A small minority of students moved this argument away from a justification for civic education into a critique of uninformed voters and contended that uneducated and uninformed voters ought not to be allowed to participate in elections. Indeed, I was surprised to hear these students advocate for some form of a poll test—even if it would result in a majority of the class (and themselves) being excluded from the election.

Two additional readings of rigorous and provocative social science research further informed our examination of the disengaged polis. The first, *Millennials Talk Politics: A Study of College Student Political Engagement* (Kiesa et al., 2007), reported on extensive focus group data collected from college students. The second, Baldassare's (2006) *California's Exclusive Electorate*, described a substantial disconnect between California voters and the population as a whole in terms of demographics and preferences on policy issues. These reports fostered a series of class discussions that substantially altered the scope and direction of the service project. The class morphed the project from a simple video voter guide into a more expansive and ambitious program including a series of public events.

The two readings affirmed students' perceptions of the need to inform and activate college students on election issues. Kiesa et al. (2007) assert that "very few students say that voting is the most beneficial vehicle for addressing public issues; in fact, voting by far receives the least support. Students overwhelmingly testify that voting is not a vehicle for change" (p. 15). My students treated this contention as a challenge rather than a barrier and maintained that information about the ballot, including the importance of the ballot issues, would convince young voters about the importance of voting. While this justified the need to focus at least in part on the campus community, and supported the creation of a video voter guide that would run on campus television, it also posed a clear dilemma: how to promote political engagement by increasing political knowledge while breaking through layers of endemic cynicism and apathy.

Redefining the Service Project

The assigned readings also encouraged students to think beyond their immediate campus surroundings: The age gap is far from the only, or even largest, disparity in rates of political participation. In California the electorate has become sufficiently distinct from the state as a whole, a subpopulation defined by high levels of income, education, and home ownership. Several students were struck by the democratic and demographic implications. If a wide gulf exists between voters and nonvoters, and education is indeed the most reliable predictor of voter participation, might it not make sense to reach beyond the campus community?

In the 2008 election, young people with college experience were about twice as likely to vote as those without (Kirby & Kawashima-Ginsberg, 2009). By conducting outreach efforts to unlikely voters, particularly those from historically underrepresented communities, could students promote participation and improve the equality of voice in elections through voter education? To achieve this objective, students recognized that voter materials would need to be disseminated in underserved communities and that posting videos to the Web would not be enough. Instead, students volunteered to attend meetings hosted by community partners throughout San Francisco. While this offered a promising avenue for engagement, it raised a broader question about how they might encourage sufficient interest in low-intensity contests like state and local ballot measures.

Kiesa et al. (2007) conclude that students find it hard to become fully conversant in public issues and crave more information. This is undoubtedly why advocates of youth political engagement propose solutions that invariably include widespread civic literacy drives through schools and universities (Levine, 2007) and similarly underpin the logic behind producing a video voter guide. My students embraced Kiesa et al.'s statement that "students are seeking opportunities for discussion that are authentic, not competitive or partisan. They appreciate discussions in which no one is trying to sell them on anything. . . . [and are] eager for opportunities to talk about issues with a diverse group of people in open and authentic ways" (pp. 4–5). In that vein, students proposed holding a series of events on campus and in the community to discuss the ballot. Through these events that were designed to be more than mere information sessions, the students hoped to encourage participants to discuss and deliberate each of the ballot measures. While I applauded their innovation, I questioned their engagement plan: Is it possible to have an authentic discussion that is the result of a fully contrived process (the formally scheduled community forum), and how might a deliberative community forum operate where the population is generally disengaged politically?

Civic Education: Democratic Dilemma Number One—Participation

Working in groups of three and four, students researched each of the state and local ballot propositions and crafted scripts that I reviewed for accuracy. The student television crew filmed the students and created an indexed video voter guide that was telecast on campus television; posted on the Internet; and disseminated in DVD form to community organizations, neighborhood centers, and local libraries. Thanks to the outstanding work of the students at the campus TV station, these voter guides were available to the community ten days before election day and broadcast on campus television during the week prior to the vote.

While students produced a generally high-quality video, their efforts to disseminate their work were not successful. It appears that the libraries, community organizations, and neighborhood associations filed away their DVDs. Concurrently, the Web materials received very few hits. And students in my other classes seemed oblivious to anything political being televised on the campus station.

Accordingly (albeit disappointingly), students gained insight into a true democratic dilemma—political engagement does depend upon some degree of participation by the polis. The students' campus colleagues and friends were not consuming political news, even in alternate electronic formats. Unfortunately, the community meetings were even less well received, both by attendees and by my students.

For the first community meeting eight students joined me in taking a van to one of our community partner sites adjacent to a public housing complex in the southeast sector of San Francisco to host a discussion of the ballot measures. In spite of considerable advertising, and a wait of 60 minutes for stragglers, only one person attended the meeting—the assistant director of the community center. Despite her best efforts to engage the students, their frustration was palpable and the conversation was superficial at best. Similarly, at the two other community meetings that week, student presenters outnumbered the audience members by at least two to one.

Back in class, I hoped to use this as a teachable moment for the students to contemplate how a civic education project might overcome demographic barriers not only in voting but also in attending and participating in public programs intended to address disparities. However, many students had drawn their own conclusions, blaming our apparent lack of success on the community partner, the faculty member who assigned the project, the students who suggested that we do community events, and ultimately the absent voters.

What had been a minority perspective, that uninformed citizens should refrain from voting, now dominated the discussion. Students expressed resentment at having to do the project and questioned whether voter education was simply a waste of time. Rather than working to increase democratic participation through civic education, a significant number of students argued that an exclusive electorate might be preferable and even might be considered more democratic.

Class debate ensued: Some students advocated limiting our outreach efforts to places likely to draw a significant number of voters and ensure success in enhancing knowledge about the ballot. Others argued these were places where our efforts would be the least needed, potentially increasing disparities. These students advocated that we stay the course and risk further disappointments. This debate illustrates the essence of a democratic dilemma: Because core democratic principles are in tension, despite our best efforts, simple solutions are unattainable.

I attempted to redirect the discussion and what we might do better in future iterations of the project to think strategically about voter engagement. Rather than assign blame or negotiate a fix, we reframed the issue and brainstormed how we might take an active part in building active participation. While a more rigorous and time-consuming voter mobilization campaign was far beyond the scope of this project, students began thinking about how they might organize their communities on campus to ensure greater turnout without relying on a privileged audience. As the students began constructing a matrix of associations and informal networks they might draw upon, we implicitly began laying the groundwork we had ignored in the broader community. And apparently this tactic worked because participation at the next campus forum climbed to 30 or 40 students. However, as this event unfolded, a second democratic dilemma emerged.

Civic Education: Democratic Dilemma Number Two—Discussion Versus Advocacy

Recall that students had expressed a preference for an authentic discussion of the issues. As the forum began, students in attendance began fidgeting. About 10 minutes in, one attendee expressed that he was not interested in having a complete discussion of each of the 26 ballot measures with all the sides presented equally; he just needed to know how to vote correctly. Others in attendance nodded in agreement and asked my students to cut to the chase and briefly present an overview.

It was abundantly clear that this civic education session would not be a civic-building enterprise. As students began to rush, the forum quickly devolved and presentation replaced deliberation as the primary mode of communication. It seems that deliberation around issues requires at least a base level of knowledge and commitment to a civic process that was not present among those in attendance. My students struggled to find their authentic voices, and the presentations quickly became uneven. Some measures were portrayed as "meaningless," and some arguments made by advocates were characterized, using various colloquialisms, as inaccurate. While students successfully avoided outright advocacy, their presentations created an unequal power dynamic.

Students faced a second democratic dilemma: Should they try to foster a robust discussion of the issues in an effort to encourage those in attendance to bring their own analysis to bear in the face of resistance, or assume the role of expert and speak authoritatively and risk undermining the democratic principles underpinning the process?

Reconsidering the Discontents of Civic Education

As with the first dilemma, the experience on campus revealed a troubling paradox: civic engagement in a disengaged environment providing an inherently noncivic process. The debriefing session in class the following week offered an opportunity to reflect upon, and learn from, the experience. Again, students expressed a desire for a quick fix and seemed genuinely astonished that I had none to offer. Instead, I redefined the problem from "How could we have made this work?" to "What are the necessary ingredients for effective political engagement?"

The question helped students gain an appreciation of the challenges associated with genuine and authentic engagement and forced them to check their assumptions about the community where they lived. Students' perspectives broadened as they moved from a deficit model of engagement to one centered around building on the enormous resources and skills present in their communities.

The lessons of this project for me were numerous and substantial, but perhaps the primary one was that some degree of tension between democratic values is inherent in any civic endeavor. Also, as an academic, I had to suppress my instincts to troubleshoot and solve and instead redirect the frustrations and redefine the issues with the intent of producing more nuanced understandings rather than more tangible successes. In the end, students left the course with more democratic tools and insights to effectively solve future civic engagement dilemmas.

References

Baldassare, M. (2006). *California's exclusive electorate.* San Francisco, CA: Public Policy Institute of California.

Kiesa, A., Orlowski, A. P., Levine, P., Both, D., Hoban, E., Kirby, E. H. et al. (2007). *Millennials talk politics: A study of college student political engagement.* College Park,

MD: Center for Information & Research on Civic Learning and Engagement. Retrieved from http://eric.ed.gov/PDFS/ED498899.pdf

Kirby, E. H., & Kawashima-Ginsberg, K. (2009). *The youth vote in 2008.* Medford, MA: Center for Information & Research on Civic Learning and Engagement. Retrieved from http://www.civicyouth.org/PopUps/FactSheets/FS_youth_Voting_2008_updated_6.22.pdf

Kirlin, M. (2002). Civic skill building: The missing component in service programs? *PS: Political Science and Politics, 35*(3), 571–575.

Levine, P. (2007). *The future of democracy: Developing the next generation of American citizens.* Medford, MA: Tufts University Press.

19

HEALTH PSYCHOLOGY AND POLITICAL ENGAGEMENT

The Why and How

Sandra A. Sgoutas-Emch

When encouraged by our office of community service-learning to participate in the California Campus Compact and the Carnegie Foundation for the Advancement of Teaching Service Learning for Political Engagement Program, I was intrigued. I routinely use service-learning in my psychology courses and wholeheartedly support it as an educational tool. As described by Colby, Beaumont, Ehrlich, and Corngold (2007), incorporating citizenship education into the curriculum can be interesting and challenging for faculty and students alike. Although experiential learning is fairly commonplace in psychology courses, the focus on political engagement is not typical in our discipline.

Interestingly, despite the fact that mental health issues and services are influenced by the political process, we rarely discuss in our courses the influence that the American Psychological Association (APA) has in shaping public policy. Everything from psychologists' rights to writing prescriptions for psychotropic medications to health care policy for the mentally ill is influenced by the legislative process. The APA, for example, routinely brings in representatives to speak to Congress about a number of mental health issues and lobbies for changes in our laws. Yet few of our psychology majors who aspire to become researchers, teachers, or therapists are fully aware of the impact psychologists have in the political arena. I decided to intentionally address this disciplinary dilemma.

Course Content and Community Partnerships

The course I selected was Health Psychology of Women and Ethnic Minorities, which focuses on how factors such as gender, race, culture, and socioeconomic status relate to one's physical health and wellness. We discuss how governmental policies and procedures can be major obstacles for people in receiving adequate health care and keeping themselves healthy. I want my students to learn how these policies and the structure of the health care system may contribute to the health disparities and outcomes that exist in our society (Fiscella, Franks, Gold, & Clancy, 2000; Lasser, Himmelstein, & Woolhandler, 2006; Mensah, Mokdad, Ford, Greenlund, & Croft, 2005). Similarly important, former students had expressed frustrations with the traditional service-learning component. They indicated a desire to be more active in the community and to make a difference. Indeed, many students who enroll in the course come from the underserved groups we examine.

My challenge was to identify the right type of placement that met the goals of our course in implementing politically engaged service-learning and how to modify the course content/assignments in a more politically focused way. Another consideration was that the placement needed to increase students' awareness of community partnerships in health care. Numerous studies have shown the importance of community and community-based programs in public health (Fitzgibbon, Stolley, Dyer, VanHorn, & Kaufer Christoffel, 2002; Kramish Campbell et al., 2007; Satterfield, Volansky, Caspersen, et al., 2003). Becoming part of the community, building trust, and working with the members of that community are all critical pieces of formulating public health interventions such as in the case of type 2 diabetes particularly in minority populations (Israel, Schulz, Parker, & Becker, 1998).

Moreover, it was essential that the students see how they as citizens could be a part of shaping government policy. Research has shown that for citizens to make informed decisions and take action in a democratic state, they must first gain the necessary skills, knowledge, and attitudes (Banks, 2004). I was hoping that by restructuring the course to be more politically focused, my students might obtain some of these citizenship qualities when it comes to the psychological health of individuals and communities.

Instructional Strategies

One of the key ways I chose to help students make the connection between the psychology class and politics was to focus on current government policies regarding women and ethnic minorities. As I was teaching the course during an election year, we examined statements made by candidates concerning these issues. Furthermore, we discussed how these statements might potentially affect policies on the health and wellness of these populations.

To frame and contextualize our discussions, I selected a variety of activities and readings, and I assigned papers that helped educate students on these connections. For example, students were asked to research government programs at the federal, state, and local levels and how they specifically affect women and ethnic minorities. The students then gave an oral presentation on programs like the Women, Infants and Children Program (WIC) and discussed what the programs were, how they were funded, and what was currently happening with the funding.

However, the community service-learning project designed for the course was the main method for helping students make connections, and it became the most powerful tool for increasing students' awareness and knowledge. Montgomery Middle School in Linda Vista, California, was the perfect community partner. The school has a diverse student body representing many ethnicities and cultures and is generally made up of lower-income families. Diversity awareness is a key objective for the course, and as Gutmann (2004) asserts, one of the primary goals of educating citizens in a democracy is to focus on issues of equity. He contends that helping people recognize that cultural differences do exist and that being tolerant of these differences are foundational for treating each other with equal respect and dignity. Similarly, Hurtado (2007) stresses that by preparing our students as citizens for a multicultural society, we can expect leadership with greater social awareness skills that may help reduce the inequities and social problems we see today.

Service-Learning Project

Montgomery Middle School received funding for a Family Success Center 2 years ago through collaboration with many partners in the Linda Vista community. The premise of the center administrators is that if families are successful, their children will perform better in school and have better attendance. However, despite its existence, use of the center to this point had been minimal, and the center was in danger of losing its funding and support. Clearly, the center was in a convenient location and had resources to provide services, so why were so few people accessing the space and services? I believed the center would be the perfect place for my students to learn about community organizations, the role politics plays in their work, and of course the role diversity plays in the structure and function of the community.

A Youth Action Team meets monthly and is composed of many community partners including people from our university, Montgomery Middle School, the San Diego Gang Commission, and the local health clinic. All these agencies and partners work together to provide support and resources for the center. Youth Action Team members graciously dedicated their time to present information to the class. Students were informed on the purpose of the center, how funding and resources were obtained, and how individuals in the community worked together to get the job done.

We also held some of our class meetings on-site so students had an opportunity to see community partners in action and be exposed to the inner workings of community collaborations. Indeed, a critical lesson we learned is that to provide effective health care it is essential to learn about the community and build trust and solicit help from community partners.

The students' primary service-learning assignment was to work with community partners on developing a survey about the Center for the community. Students helped design and distribute the surveys that focused on gaining information about knowledge of, attitudes toward, and use of the Family Success Center services. The survey included community demographic questions. These data were especially eye-opening for the students by giving a collective picture of who lives in the community. The class then analyzed the data, and students worked in groups to develop new ideas for attracting people to the center.

To better understand the politics of community work, students were required to attend at least two community meetings that focused on a health care issue for the residents of Linda Vista. Interestingly, politicians (or their surrogates) often came to these meetings to update community members about current legislative action. Students had the opportunity to hear from politicians at the local, state, and national levels (U.S. Senate and House of Representatives). In fact, the Linda Vista Collaboration, a health care collaborative of local community partners, specifically devoted one of its monthly meetings to health care policy issues because of the students' project.

Making Course and Community Policy Connections

During class, students were expected to report to their classmates what they heard and observed at the meetings and to explain the psychology-policy implications. One such student discussion focused on a county health meeting where it was announced that all funding for teen pregnancy programming was going to be either eliminated or severely reduced. At the meeting, the head of the local teen health clinic discussed statistics on teen pregnancy in the area and the impact these budget cuts would potentially have on teen pregnancy rates. Upon hearing this report, students were upset that funding was being eliminated for programs that appeared to be effective. As illustrated by the student journal reflection below, it cemented the connections between the course and policies and budgets:

> At the last meeting of Healthy Initiatives there was a lot of discussion about the future of these health organizations now that the budget cuts have occurred. The programs that have to do with young adults and their sexual health have been cut by the state and the individuals that used to work for these programs must find other jobs. This is an example of how even with people available, if funds are not available programs cannot be created and continued. These meetings have shown me that the difficulty with community planning does depend on how well the event is organized, but more importantly if the funds are not available then nothing can be done.

Generally, students began the semester with little awareness of the interdependent relationships among psychology, politics, and individual and community health. But slowly, as students completed the readings and research, participated in the course discussions, and engaged in the service-learning site and project, they learned there is a deep and important connection, as shown in the following:

> For me, I found it hard to really understand how an issue might affect me or someone else because I personally had or may not even be in a situation where the issues would affect me. I now know a lot of issues that I will face in the future are being shaped by the decisions our political leaders make now, but it was hard for me to fully comprehend it. I think it will take more time and more researching and reading about the issues to understand them completely.

By becoming more informed, people can understand where help is needed and what needs to be improved. Some people have no idea about the inequalities minorities are facing in the health care field and it is important to update them. It is important to get out and vote.

In conclusion, intentionally integrating political engagement fulfilled my objectives for the health psychology course, which included helping students understand the importance of community in health and wellness, the role of individuals in our democracy, and the existence of health disparities in our system. Moreover, it helped students realize how to apply and take action using their psychology knowledge and skills for the improved health of individuals and communities.

References

Banks, J. A. (Ed.). (2004). *Diversity and citizenship education: Global perspectives*. San Francisco, CA: Jossey-Bass.

Colby, A., Beaumont, E., Ehrlich, T., & Corngold, J. (2007). *Educating for democracy*. San Francisco, CA: Jossey-Bass.

Fiscella, K., Franks, P., Gold, M. R., & Clancy, C. M. (2000). Addressing socioeconomic, racial, and ethnic disparities in health care. *JAMA, 283*, 2579–2584.

Fitzgibbon, M. L., Stolley, M. R., Dyer, A. R., VanHorn, L., & Kaufer Christoffel, K. (2002). A community-based obesity prevention program for minority children: Rationale and study design for hip-hop to health. *Preventive Medicine, 34*(2), 289–297.

Gutmann, A. (2004). Unity and diversity in democratic multicultural educations: Creative and destructive tensions. In J. A. Banks (Ed.), *Diversity and citizenship education: Global perspectives* (pp. 71–96). San Francisco, CA: Jossey-Bass.

Hurtado, S. (2007). Linking diversity with the educational and civic missions of higher education. *Review of Higher Education, 30*(2), 185–196.

Israel, B. A., Schulz, A. J., Parker, E. A., & Becker, A. B. (1998). Review of community-based research: Assessing partnership approaches to improve public health. *Annual Review of Public Health, 19*, 173–202.

Kramish Campbell, M., Hudson, M. A., Resnicow, K., Blakeney, N., Paxton, A., & Baskin, M. (2007). Church-based health promotion interventions: Evidence and lessons learned. *Annual Review of Public Health, 28*, 213–214.

Lasser, K. E., Himmelstein, D. U., & Woolhandler, S. (2006). Access to care, health status, and health disparities in the United States and Canada: Results of a cross-national population-based survey. *American Journal of Public Health, 96*(7), 1300–1307.

Mensah, G. A., Mokdad, A. H., Ford, E. S., Greenlund, K. J., & Croft, J. B. (2005). State of disparities in cardiovascular health in the United States. *Circulation, 111*, 1233–1241.

Satterfield, D. W., Volansky, M., Caspersen, et al. (2003). Community-based lifestyle interventions to prevent type 2 diabetes. *Diabetes Care, 26*(9), 2643–2652.

20

TO REFORM OR TO EMPOWER?

Asian American Studies and Education for Critical Consciousness

Kathleen S. Yep

I felt very isolated from the [high school students] today. . . . It just felt like a lot of the lesson plan was us telling them what was wrong with their communities and why they should be changed. . . . I feel that my expectations of [their] experience(s) . . . is [*sic*] absolutely a reflection of my own white and class privilege, and there's a way in which that's painful for me to admit.

—College student in an Asian American studies course

T his is one college student's reflection on a community partnership with incarcerated high school students in an Asian American studies course. It highlights the complexities that arise in encouraging civic and political engagement in higher education and the dynamic interplay of individual actions and social forces that can lead to inequities. Philosophers of education have argued that the purpose of education is to create citizens who will serve society. Whereas Plato (1961) and Aristotle (1997) viewed education as facilitating the knowledge of goodness and thus a good society, John Stuart Mill (1867/1997) contended that education should encourage civic engagement, and John Locke (1880/1997) argued for character building in education. Many higher education scholars, such as Butin (2008) and

Cuban and Hayes (1997), have reframed civic engagement and service-learning to have explicit purposes for political engagement and the creation of social equity.

Similarly, Asian Americanists interrogate the notion of citizenry by situating it in the historical contexts of social inequalities such as racialized incarceration at the Angel Island Immigration Station off the coast of San Francisco in the early 1900s, the World War II imprisonment of Japanese American citizens, and the 1986 California constitutional amendment establishing English as the official language (Nakano Glenn, 2004; Ngai, 2005). Consequently, scholars such as Luibheid (2002) shifted the notion of citizenship from a neutral, duty-bound relationship to the state to a conflictual one. Simultaneously, Asian American studies reframed the goals of higher education. Emerging from a multiracial social movement in the late 1960s, Asian American studies was organized around the principles of community engagement, social justice, and democratic pedagogies (Kim, 2000; Tang, 2008). With these community-based origins, the field of Asian American studies emphasizes creating a more equitable society rather than molding active citizens through experiential learning. Many Asian American studies scholars, such as Mohanty (2003) and Omatsu (1999), have argued that education is a highly contested terrain in which teaching and learning are not neutral. Instead, systems of power and privilege are strengthened and challenged in educational environments. As such, for many Asian Americanists the community is neither an object of study to be fixed nor a site of academic tourism for college students (Camacho, 2004; Cruz, 1990). Rather, the purpose of community-based learning is to empower the college students and the community to create a more just society together (Kim-Ju, Mark, Cohen, Garcia-Santiago, & Nguyen, 2008; Lin, Suyemoto, & Kiang, 2009).

In this chapter I discuss my Asian American studies community-based learning class where the college students initially emphasized reforming community members to become "better citizens," and thus replicated unequal positions of privilege in the community partnership (Forbes, Garber, Kensigner, & Slagter, 1999; Rosenberger, 2000). While I designed the course drawing from political engagement and democratic organizing principles of Asian American studies to shift the students from a public service framework to a social justice model (Bickford & Reynolds, 2002), assisting students along this continuum is no easy task. This teaching case shows how becoming active citizens is inextricably bound with interrogating power and privilege and how problem-posing pedagogies in Asian American studies courses can be a vehicle for creating social justice and empowering relationships in community-based learning.

Teaching Context

My Asian American studies course compares various nonviolent social change tactics and philosophies and examines the interplay among structural, symbolic, and individual violence (Bourdieu, 1989; Gilligan, 1996). At the private liberal arts college where I teach, I carry forward the community-based origins of Asian American studies by partnering with the college's Community Engagement Center and a high school at a local juvenile detention center. Managed by the county probation department, the detention center houses about 225 young men who range in age from 13 to 17 and whose average length of incarceration is six months.

At the beginning of each semester, I attempt to prepare my college students to reflect critically on the social context and power dynamics of working with incarcerated students (Cress, Collier, Reitenauer, & Associates, 2005). In addition to attending a workshop about the ethics of community-based learning, the college students write about the history of the prison system in the United States. They also read poetry written by some of the detention center high school students and texts on the politics and problematics of service-learning with incarcerated populations specifically (Davis, 2003; Meisel, 2008).

Reinforcing Hierarchies

Typically, college students in the course thrive in the traditional modes of exposition and analysis of the readings (Kolb & Kolb, 2005). However, once students begin their written community engagement reflections, the disjunctures between theory and practice usually begin to emerge. Reading about power and structural violence at an abstract conceptual level is fundamentally different from understanding such concepts at the juvenile detention center. Initially the college students treated the concepts of power and violence as something outside the classroom, including their interactions with the community partners. Although they acted compassionately and were highly motivated learners, their written reflections and in-class comments often reinforced social inequalities by using deficit-based explanations for the high school students' incarceration. The college students framed the high school students as a social problem and struggled with how to view them as co-learners and co-teachers (Wallace, 2000; Ward & Wolf-Wendel, 2000).

As an example, a student named "Amy" had good intentions but emphasized changing the individual choices of the high school students:

> From my own impressions and preformed notions, everything about the high school seemed violent—the atmosphere, many of the students. . . . Currently, the purpose of prison seems to be to punish deviants and remove them from society. However, shouldn't the overall goal be to teach and reform them, so that they can return to society as constructive members? . . . I want to teach them to make better choices.

Amy referred to the structural violence these high school students face, yet she stressed "working on" the high school students. Although she critiques the punitive model of the prison system, she does not frame the high school students as allies who have their own standpoints and agency (Smith, 1990). This perspective of repairing the high school students, and thus dehumanizing them, mirrors the gap many organizers face between teaching students about social inequalities and motivating community members to practice social and political engagement.

Community Mapping Strategy

By reducing the high school students to objects to be mended, the college students erased their own positions of privilege and reproduced existing systems of inequality. The outcome was that their behavior toward the high school students maintained an air of elitism and charity that made for forced and awkward interpersonal dynamics with the high school students. In addition, the college students tended to explain the high school students' academic struggles by pointing out the attributes or resources the students or students' families lacked (Ginwright & Cammarota, 2002).

To address these problematic patterns, I incorporated a community mapping exercise formulated by Michael James (personal communication, August 8, 2004) and based on the earlier work of Paulo Freire (1998). Influenced by Freire's "problem-posing pedagogies" (pp. 32–33), the community mapping exercise draws from student knowledge as the foundation to highlight the impact of social processes on individuals and the influence of individuals on society.

Noting the mapping discussion might trigger negative emotions and memories, I reminded students of my office hours and highlighted counseling resources they could access if needed. As a first mapping activity, students created a visual representation of their childhood neighborhood. After giving some examples, I asked them to draw the institutions and stakeholders in their neighborhood. Then, as a class, we defined structural violence, and I invited students to think of illustrations of structural violence in their community.

Initially, the students struggled to identify institutional violence in their own lives so they formed pairs to assist each other. One duo drew an armored tank and barbed wire to represent the Vietnam War and one of the pair's families' experience in a refugee camp. We then examined the causes of structural violence. For example, the same pair drew a capitol building and a flag to symbolize the role of the state, and they drew televisions to represent civil society and ideologies. The students finished their maps by drawing two possible interventions to address the institutional violence. The same duo drew a family dinner with conversation bubbles to symbolize sharing stories about experiences in refugee camps, and books to represent documenting the hidden histories of Cambodian refugees.

At the next class we explored how the students might map their communities in conjunction with the high school students. Several of the students argued the maps objectified the high school students. Amy and others expressed discomfort about revealing their relative privilege to the high school students and questioned the relevance of sharing this information. Several students grappled with the realization that even though they had completed readings and written reflections about social inequities in communities, they had never asked the high school students about their lives nor told them anything about their own.

Musil (2009) contends that for college students to move from good intentions to informed social participants, they need to make their own lives transparent and enter a mutually respectful relationship with community partners as co-learners and co-teachers. Doing so means directly engaging with different positions of privilege. Despite the students' reservations, I encouraged them to pair with a high school student at the detention center, share their stories, and draw each other's neighborhoods. Some used similar visual maps, while others used the spoken word or written poetry.

Learning Outcomes

By the end of the semester, the college students showed a paradigm shift from "fixing" the high school students to examining why social injustices exist. When the college students entered the community partnership with relatively unexamined privilege, they overlooked how these different social locations might affect their community-based learning and social analysis (Nieto, 2004). Through the mapping exercise, the college students viewed their experiences from new perspectives allowing them to analyze different social positions and how these shape individual and group trajectories. As Amy explained:

> The high school is a juvenile detention center for teenage boys, and practically all serving time there are ethnic minorities, most of which are either Black or Latino. Now, I am *keenly* aware of my privileged socio-economic status and place in society, which I largely took for granted before. I clearly understand that it is not an exaggeration to say that Blacks and Latinos are victims of institutionalized racism in the criminal justice system, a claim that I may have challenged somewhat before.

The individual mapping and collaborative mapping exercises with the high school students helped the college students learn about power, not only as an abstract concept but how and why it manifests itself in daily life for different groups of people from various social locations. In addition, students gained insight into the interconnections between democracy and collaboration, an essential skill for political engagement. Rather than the college students' telling the high school students about structural violence or to be nonviolent, both groups learned to analyze social locations through dialogue, more closely realizing Freire's (1973/2005) ultimate goal of education as a collective and liberatory process. In fact, the idea of educational reciprocity translated into learning to share with and listen to the high school students. At the end of the semester, Amy reflected on this newly created democratic and reciprocal learning environment:

> It is crucial to understand that learning from others is a major piece. At the high school, everyone was a teacher, and I learned a great amount from

my fellow classmates and students. As volunteers for the poetry program, we intentionally made the classroom an egalitarian environment. . . . Thus, to maximize the educational value for all, we broke down the traditional power dynamics between teacher and student. . . . This was precisely our aim in the poetry program, and I have found that I, too, have acquired many new insights from speaking and working with the [high school students].

Asian American Studies and Reframing Civic Engagement

As Featherstone and Ishibashi (2006) noted, the process of listening and mapping is a powerful strategy for creating connection and collaboration as part of a larger project of social change. In this way, students learned that democratic participation is not only a physical act, such as voting, but also a relational process in the context of social inequalities. After all, key elements of being politically active are creating dialogue and democratic ways of problem solving. As Amy explained, nonviolent social change is a continual process of reflection and action:

> I began to view nonviolent social change, not just as a short-term practice that is applied solely in large social movements but as a way of life, if you so choose . . . nonviolent social change is a process of transformation. . . . The ongoing element is key.

As this teaching case attests, Asian American studies and the integration of critical pedagogies can reframe and retool students' preparation for civic engagement. College students' closing reflections indicated that the mapping exercise was a strategic tool for interrogating social locations and identifying sources of individual agency instead of feeling overwhelmed by the complexities of racial discrimination and other social injustices. Moreover, it created a reciprocal platform for interpersonal connections with the high school students so that both groups were empowered to analyze social contradictions in society. In fact, many college students noted feeling bolstered in their lifelong commitment to political engagement, as exemplified by Amy: "I am now more willing to be an active participant in the nonviolent social change process . . . as I am now better equipped to fully gauge the implications."

Within Asian American studies, citizenship and civic engagement are situated in the historically contested relationship between the state and Asian

American and Pacific Islander communities. As such, the Asian American studies' goal of civic engagement departs from the liberal democratic paradigm of social obligations connected to citizenship, such as performing good works in society (May, 1999). Instead, Asian American studies and problem-posing pedagogies conceptualize civic engagement as collectively identifying and interrogating social inequalities. According to Giroux (2001), this includes mediating the material and social consequences of privilege that manifest themselves in daily life, including community-based learning partnerships. Developing dialogical relationships and understanding the social contexts of individuals are crucial to practicing democracy and creating a more just society. The integration of problem-posing pedagogies, such as community mapping, into Asian American studies courses can be a strategy for realizing those goals.

References

Aristotle. (1997). Nicomachean ethics (D. Ross, Trans.). In S. M. Cahn, (Ed.), *Classic and contemporary readings in the philosophy of education* (pp. 111–131). New York, NY: McGraw-Hill.

Bickford, D. M., & Reynolds, N. (2002). Activism and service-learning: Reframing volunteerism as acts of dissent. *Pedagogy: Critical Approaches to Teaching Literature, Language, Composition and Culture, 2,* 229–254.

Bourdieu, P. (1989). Social space and symbolic power. *Sociological Theory, 7*(1), 14–25.

Butin, D. W. (2008). *Service-learning and social justice education.* New York, NY: Routledge.

Camacho, M. M. (2004). Power and privilege: Community service learning in Tijuana. *Michigan Journal of Community Service Learning, 10*(3), 31–42.

Cress, C. M., Collier, P. J., Reitenauer, V. L., & Associates (2005). *Learning through serving: A student guidebook for service-learning across the disciplines.* Sterling, VA: Stylus.

Cruz, N. (1990). A challenge to the notion of service. In J. C. Kendall (Ed.), *Combining service and learning: A resource book for community and public service* (pp. 321–323). Raleigh, NC: National Society for Internships and Experiential Education.

Cuban, S., & Hayes, E. (1997). Border pedagogy: A critical framework for service learning. *Michigan Journal of Community Service Learning, 4,* 72–80.

Davis, A. (2003). *Are prisons obsolete?* New York, NY: Seven Stories Press.

Featherstone, E., & Ishibashi, J. (2006). Oreos and bananas: Conversations on whiteness. In V. Lea & J. Helfand (Eds.), *Identifying race and transforming whiteness in the classroom* (pp. 87–108). New York, NY: Peter Lang.

Forbes, K., Garber, L., Kensigner, L., & Slagter, J. T. (1999). Punishing pedagogy: The failings of forced volunteerism. *Women's Studies Quarterly, 7*(3–4), 158–168.

Freire, P. (1998). *Pedagogy of freedom: Ethics, democracy and civic courage* (P. Clarke, Trans.). New York: Rowman & Littlefield.

Freire, P. (2005). *Education for critical consciousness.* New York, NY: Continuum. (Original work published 1973)

Gilligan, J. (1996). *Violence: Reflections on a national epidemic.* New York, NY: Vintage Books.

Ginwright, S., & Cammarota, J. (2002). New terrain in youth development: The promise of a social justice approach. *Social Justice, 29*(4), 82–95.

Giroux, H. (2001). *Theory and resistance in education.* Santa Barbara, CA: Praeger Press.

Kim, N. (2000). The general survey course on Asian American women: Transformative education and Asian American feminist pedagogy. *Journal of Asian American Studies, 3*(1), 37–65.

Kim-Ju, G., Mark, G., Cohen, R., Garcia-Santiago, O., & Nguyen, P. (2008). Community mobilization and its application to youth violence prevention. *American Journal of Preventive Medicine, 34* (Suppl. 3), S5–S12.

Kolb, D. A., & Kolb, A. Y. (2005). Learning styles and learning spaces: Enhancing experiential learning in higher education. *Academy of Management Learning and Education, 4*(2), 193–212.

Lin, N., Suyemoto, K., & Kiang, P. N. (2009). Education as catalyst for intergenerational refugee family communication about war and trauma. *Communication Disorders Quarterly, 30,* 195–207.

Locke, J. (1997). Some thoughts concerning education. In S. M. Cahn (Ed.), *Classic and contemporary readings in the philosophy of education* (pp. 145–161). New York, NY: McGraw-Hill.

Luibheid, E. (2002). *Entry denied: Controlling sexuality at the border.* Minneapolis, MN: University of Minnesota Press.

May, S. (1999). *Critical multiculturalism: Rethinking multicultural and antiracist education.* Oxon, UK: RoutledgeFalmer.

Meisel, J. S. (2008). The ethics of observing: Confronting the harm of experiential learning. *Teaching Sociology, 36,* 196–210.

Mill, J. S. (1997). Inaugural address at St. Andrews. In S. M. Cahn (Ed.), *Classic and contemporary readings in the philosophy of education* (pp. 224–260). New York, NY: McGraw-Hill.

Mohanty, C. (2003). *Feminism without borders: Decolonizing theory, practicing solidarity.* Durham, NC: Duke University Press.

Musil, C. (2009). Educating students for personal and social responsibility: The civic learning spiral. In B. Jacoby & Associates (Eds.), *Civic engagement in higher education: Concepts and practices* (pp. 49–68). San Francisco, CA: Jossey-Bass.

Nakano Glenn, E. (2004). *Unequal freedom: How race and gender shaped American citizenship.* Cambridge, MA: Harvard University Press.

Ngai, M. (2005). *Impossible subjects: Illegal aliens and the making of modern America.* Princeton, NJ: Princeton University Press.

Nieto, S. (2004). *Affirming diversity: The sociopolitical context of multicultural education* (4th ed.). New York, NY: Allyn & Bacon.

Omatsu, G. (1999). Teaching for social change: Learning how to afflict the comfortable and comfort the afflicted. *Loyola of Los Angeles Review, 32,* 791–797.

Plato. (1961). The republic (P. Shorey, Trans.). In E. Hamilton & H. Cairns (Eds.), *The collected dialogues of Plato* (pp. 575–845). Princeton, NJ: Princeton University Press.

Rocheleau, J. (2004). Theoretical roots of service-learning: Progressive education and the development of citizenship. In B. W. Speck & S. L. Hoppe (Eds.), *Service-learning: History, theory, and issues* (pp. 3–22). Westport, CT: Praeger.

Rosenberger, C. (2000). Beyond empathy: Developing critical consciousness through service learning. In C. R. O'Grady (Ed.), *Integrating service learning and multicultural education in colleges and universities* (pp. 25–43). Mahwah, NJ: Erlbaum.

Smith, D. (1990). *The ideological practice of sociology, the conceptual practices of power: A feminist sociology of knowledge.* Toronto, Canada: University of Toronto Press.

Tang, S. S. (2008). Community-centered research as knowledge/capacity building in immigrant and refugee communities. In C. Hale (Ed.), *Engaging contradictions: Theory, politics, and methods of activist scholarship* (pp. 237–263). Berkeley, CA: University of California Press.

Wallace, J. (2000). A popular education model for college in community. *American Behavioral Scientist, 43*(5), 756–766.

Ward, K., & Wolf-Wendel, L. (2000). Community-centered service learning: Moving from doing for to doing with. *American Behavioral Scientist, 43*(5), 767–780.

PART SIX

EVALUATING DEMOCRATIC PROCESS AND PROGRESS

ASSESSMENT OF EXPECTED AND UNEXPECTED SERVICE-LEARNING OUTCOMES

Christine M. Cress

The community partner for a small-business development organization calls you at the end of the semester to inform you that the marketing plan students developed contains multiple editing errors and loading it onto its website crashed its system. You read in students' journals that the social service agency director is rarely at the site and relies on the students to show up and entertain the at-risk schoolkids. Your department chair calls you into her office and recommends you spend less time being a do-gooder and more time on your research. You leave work wondering if all your efforts have mattered and reconsidering whether to engage again in service-learning.

As the contributors to this book indicate, teaching service-learning is hard work and fraught with difficulties. Yet, just like international travel, which entails negotiating a myriad of details about foreign places and unfamiliar people, service-learning is a journey to the unknown full of unexpected challenges and rich with unexpected outcomes.

In the end, the marketing plan, after further editing, actually resulted in a monthly neighborhood street festival garnering local merchants more income and an increased sense of a connected community. The social services director was able to meet with local foundations because he could rely on the college students to supervise the children's activities. The result was a $10,000 grant to build a new rock-climbing wall in the facility. You gave your department chair a copy of the paper you presented at your last national conference highlighting how service-learning, as an engaged pedagogical tool, increased student learning of academic content. And she was impressed with your scholarship of teaching.

The service-learning research literature is quite extensive concerning student learning outcomes and the impact on community health and vitality. Still, more research is needed to understand institutional and community contexts, the nuances of pedagogical practices, and short- and long-term community improvement, to name a few (Cress, Burack, Giles, Elkins, & Stevens, 2010). A key task facing faculty is to evaluate the process: tracking, recording, gathering data, and analyzing experiences so future service-learning programs can be intellectually deeper and more effective. What worked for the students (or not)? What worked for the community partner (or not)? And what worked for you as the instructor (or not)?

The following section describes an evaluation framework that can facilitate the assessment design process. This is followed by more examples of quantitative and qualitative approaches including assessment of one's own teaching experience. Finally, additional suggestions are offered for utilizing service-learning sites as points for engaged scholarship, which can lead to dissemination and publication of new knowledge and greater opportunities for solving community issues.

Assessment Framework

Gelmon, Holland, Driscoll, Spring, and Kerrigan (2001) assert that assessment should help us articulate our learning to others in an effort to improve educational processes. In essence, we should engage in assessment practices not just to get statistical data or hear a story, but so this new information can be used to strategize actions that enhance teaching, learning, growth, and change. For them, the assessment learning cycle (see Figure 21.1) is a continual process involving four phases:

1. Observe and understand service-learning program and project experiences.
2. Collect data about these experiences.
3. Analyze the data using appropriate theoretical, conceptual, and research models.

4. Identify and implement strategic actions to improve courses, programs, and projects.

Probably your own teaching and professional work has already included assessment for learning and action:

- Calculation of student test results indicated to you that a lesson or section you taught was not fully understood. Therefore, you adjusted your teaching approach and future testing process.
- In reviewing exit surveys of graduating students, you realized that professional knowledge objectives critical to their career success were lacking. Therefore, you and your faculty colleagues reexamined class content against a rubric grid of professional objectives and made changes to syllabi accordingly.
- Perhaps you have already tried to incorporate community-based learning activities into your class, but interviews with students following the experience made you feel that academic content was overly sacrificed for service; thus, you're reading this book for more ideas to implement!

These are examples of using assessment as a learning cycle, especially if further assessment is used to analyze the effectiveness of implemented changes.

Gelmon et al. (2001) also offer ideas for an assessment matrix that can be helpful to service-learning methodological design. Many students, as well as faculty, may be unfamiliar with assessment techniques. Based on Gelmon et al. (2001) and Gelmon, Agre-Kippenhan, and Cress (2005), a parsimonious model is offered below that can be learned easily and applied as part of either faculty or student service-learning responsibilities for assessing impact and outcomes.

There are three basic dimensions to the service-learning assessment framework: Concept, Indicator, and Method, as shown in Table 21.1, Service-Learning Assessment Model: Assessing Community Impact. In the example, assessing the impact of service-learning on community is applied to the assessment model and outlined below:

- Concept: What do we want to know? The key information needed is impact on the community organization as a result of the service-learning partnership.

- Indicator: How will we know it? An outcome could be the type of clients who are served; a benchmark might be new funding generated for the community partner through grant writing.
- Method: What is the evidence? Data sources could be tracking actual number of clients assisted or number of student service hours. Similarly, increased fiscal and equipment resources are evidence of impact.

To further understand the service-learning assessment model in practice, take, for example, Catherine Gabor's assessment approach in Chapter 22. The Concept she wants to evaluate is student understanding of writing as a political act. What would be the Indicator? Students' articulation of how they used writing for leveraging political actions and policy decisions. What

FIGURE 21.1
Assessment Learning Cycle

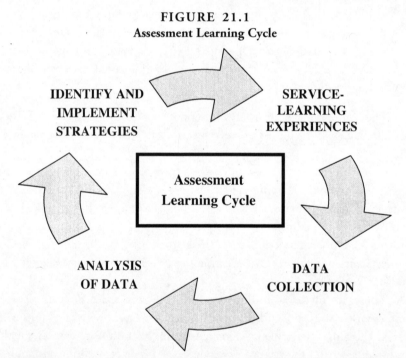

Source: Adapted from *Assessing Service-Learning and Civic Engagement: Principles and Techniques*, by S. B. Gelmon, B. A. Holland, A. Driscoll, A. Spring, & S. Kerrigan, 2001. Providence, RI: Campus Compact; and Beyond a Grade: Are We Making a Difference? In C. M. Cress, P. J. Collier, V. L. Reitenauer, & Associates (Eds.), *Learning Through Serving: A Student Guidebook for Service-Learning Across the Disciplines*, by S. B. Gelmon, S. Agre-Kippenhan, & C. Cress, 2005, pp. 125–138. Sterling, VA: Stylus.

TABLE 21.1
Service-Learning Assessment Model: Assessing Community Impact

CONCEPT Key information	INDICATOR(S) Benchmarks/outcomes	METHOD(S) Data sources
I. Impact of service-learning on community organization	1. Clients served	A. Number of clients assisted B. Number of student service hours
	2. New funding generated	A. New grant money received B. New equipment donations

Source: Based on work by Gelmon, Holland, Driscoll, Spring, and Kerrigan (2001); and Gelmon, Agre-Kippenham, and Cress (2005).

would be the Evidence? Students would make statements and provide descriptions of their service-learning writing as a political act during post-class interviews with the instructor (see Table 21.2).

Gabor's primary assessment concept is the fundamental purpose of her service-learning course: expanding student writing skills as a tool for positive community impact. However, rather than assessing the writing itself, Gabor is interested in how writing becomes a conscious demonstration of political beliefs put into action. In essence, how does writing add to an individual definition of one's self as a democratic citizen? For Gabor, that is the indicator that the linkage between the writing course and political engagement was successful. Evidence (or documenting data) of this linkage was gathered by Gabor not just through reading student writing but through qualitative focus groups and interviews. She hoped students would not just articulate these insights in writing but also verbalize them and thereby more deeply embed their understanding of writing as a political act. Ultimately, Gabor comes to realize that her assessment method is a form of engaged scholarship and engaged teaching (as defined by Boyer, 1990). Based on her data analysis, she makes iterative changes for improvement to her syllabus to better facilitate student reflection and processing, in sum, the cycle of assessment for learning.

TABLE 21.2
Service-Learning Assessment Model: Assessing Student Understanding

CONCEPT Key information	INDICATOR(S) Benchmarks/outcomes	METHOD(S) Data sources
I. Student understanding of writing as a political act	1. Student-written statements describing writing as a political act	A. Student class papers B. Student journal reflections
	2. Student verbal statements describing writing as a political act	A. Student class presentations B. Student interviews C. Student focus groups

Source: Based on work by Gelmon, Holland, Driscoll, Spring, and Kerrigan (2001); and Gelmon, Agre-Kippenham, and Cress (2005).

Engaged Scholarship

Similarly, Laura Nichols, Fernando Cázares, and Angelica Rodriguez in Chapter 23 describe their assessment processes as engaged scholarship as well as a sociology inquiry tool for teaching students how to collect, assess, and disseminate data. Nichols uses a pre- and posttest survey to measure student growth on her primary concept: political efficacy. That is, how do students view themselves as democratic citizens with its attendant responsibilities for involvement? The indicators in this case are student responses of agreement and disagreement to various statements as provided on the surveys, which is the method of evidence (see Table 21.3).

It is notable that while students scored themselves quite high on political efficacy on the pretest survey, they still showed gains in political efficacy on the posttest as a result of the service-learning course. This is probably because students were actively engaged in the collection of quantitative and qualitative data concerning the needs of the homeless in their community. At the outset of the class, students had to grapple with their own assessment methodologies including how to interact with and solicit information from homeless individuals. Students' solved problems on issues of human subjects' rights and confidentiality as well as data analysis and dissemination concerns regarding validity, reliability, and policy recommendations to city leaders for

TABLE 21.3

Service-Learning Assessment Model: Assessing Student Understanding

CONCEPT Key information	INDICATOR(S) Benchmarks/outcomes	METHOD(S) Data sources
I. Student understanding of political efficacy	1. Student agreement that they view themselves as having the skills and interests for involving themselves in community issues	A. Pretest survey B. Posttest survey

Source: Based on work by Gelmon, Holland, Driscoll, Spring, and Kerrigan (2001); and Gelmon, Agre-Kippenham, and Cress (2005).

change. As Nichols, Cázares, and Rodriguez assert, dealing with actual data dilemmas gave students real knowledge and skills for political efficacy.

Other Assessment Considerations

Identifying the outcomes of service-learning to improve teaching, learning, and impacts is reliant upon a number of additional considerations. Begin with a simple assessment model as described previously and then review and expand it as your (and your students') knowledge, skill, and confidence increase. For example, if you can access entering student data from your institutional research office, it would be interesting to see how students with previous service-learning experience (in high school or at another college) fare in their learning outcomes as compared to those who are engaging in service-learning for the very first time. Alternatively, if you can access exit student survey data from graduating seniors you may be able to track the retention and degree of success of your service-learning students over time.

Some service-learning faculty have a wealth of knowledge and skills in assessment methods while others need new ideas, tips, and strategies for evaluating outcomes. Following are a number of additional suggestions and issues to consider in your methodological design to ensure reliability and validity of results and to fully realize assessment as a learning cycle.

Participant consent and confidentiality. All data collection should be conducted according to stringent ethical and legal regulations, including participants' right to decline involvement and their right to the strictest confidence.

Most colleges' institutional review boards (IRBs) protect human subjects' rights. Normally, any data that are collected beyond the scope of a class project, such as those used for public reports, presentations, or publications, must first be approved as a justifiable research project by the college IRB. If in doubt about it being merely a class project, check with your IRB committee or institutional research office before proceeding.

Cultural contexts and sensitivity. The usefulness of data for leveraging positive change is dependent on their legitimacy. Are the data accurate? Are they representative of an individual experience? A group's experience? A community's experience? How are data collected? The means of obtaining survey responses or getting answers to questions is just as important as how data are analyzed and communicated. Survey items and interview questions should be pilot tested against language, cultural, and experiential differences. Moreover, careful thought should go into the human dynamic of data collector and data responder; all the nuances of interpersonal and nonverbal communication can come into play regarding position, power, and privilege.

For example, should a middle-class White student interview in English the Spanish-speaking parents of middle school students who scored low on a language proficiency test? While collection of family background data may be essential for developing service-learning support programs, there are multiple arguments for and against this kind of scenario. Asking (and answering) cultural context and sensitivity questions during the assessment design process can help ensure that appropriate data training, collection, and analysis occur.

Poorly designed questions. Another reason to pilot test assessment protocols is that often the best of our intentions are just not conceptually clear. The terminology we think conveys an important idea is misunderstood.

For example, take the following statement, "The experience enhanced my civic capacity skills." As the instructor who wrote the survey item, I know precisely what I have in mind: The service-learning course increased students' sense of themselves as community change agents. But multiple questions come to mind for the student respondent:

- What experience? The tour at the youth correction facility or the guest speaker from the Latino community center?

- What does *enhanced* mean? I was already a good writer so the service-learning reflection journals, especially because they were informally rather than formally written, didn't really improve my writing.
- What is a civic capacity skill? I tutored kids but I didn't register people to vote.

Pilot testing protocol and getting feedback from others can help ensure that our concepts and indicators provide direct evidence of the outcomes we want to measure. For those of us using the data for engaged scholarship or future grant applications, substantiating our methods is critical because most editors and grant reviewers want evidence that our research is rigorous and our findings are applicable to broad audiences, institutions, and organizations.

Stakeholders and dissemination. The assessment process inherently includes dilemmas of who should be told what about whom. Should a city council receive neighborhood assets data from White students who collected it in a primarily African American section of the city? Or should the African American Community Council present the data collaboratively with the students and faculty?

Moreover, how recommendations for improvement get conveyed can have a critical impact on relationships. In one service-learning course, students invited the community partners to their final presentations, which resulted in embarrassing and angering the agency representatives when students harshly criticized their practices and policies.

And many instructors are well aware that new service-learning courses often result in initially less-positive student course evaluations than traditionally taught lecture-type classes (Cress, Kerrigan, & Reitenauer, 2003). Explaining this to promotion and tenure committees whose members are primarily interested in increased teaching evaluation trend lines is a challenge and an educational opportunity for extending one's teaching and scholarship. Fortunately, more and more professional discipline and academic associations are recognizing the pedagogical value of service-learning. As such, getting a service-learning-based presentation accepted at a conference and getting service-learning research published in nationally ranked peer-reviewed journals are becoming increasingly common as educators and scholars recognize that civic engagement leads to student academic success (Cress et al., 2010).

Community-Based Research

Service-learning is rich with opportunities for assessing teaching, learning, and impact—whether the individual, class, college, or community is affected. As noted earlier, some faculty link their assessment methods with colleagues to create larger data sets for more statistical power and detailed analysis of variables. Others work with their institutional research offices to connect entering and exiting student survey data in tracking retention and graduation rates. Still others collaborate with community partners to write research grants and investigate new approaches for solving community challenges.

Certainly, the social, economic, environmental, and political issues facing our colleges and communities will not be solved overnight or through one service-learning course. But instructors and colleges that embed themselves as anchors of learning and research in the community are quite likely to facilitate and make evident individual student growth and improved community vitality (Coalition of Urban Serving Universities, 2010).

References

Boyer, E. L. (1990). *Scholarship reconsidered: Priorities of the professoriate.* San Francisco, CA: Jossey-Bass.

Coalition of Urban Serving Universities. (2010). *Urban universities: Anchors generating prosperity for America's cities.* Washington, DC: Author.

Cress, C. M., Burack, C., Giles, D. E., Jr., Elkins, J., & Stevens, M. C. (2010). *A promising connection: Increasing college access and success through civic engagement.* Boston, MA: Campus Compact.

Cress, C. M., Kerrigan, S., & Reitenauer, V. (Fall, 2003). Making community-based learning meaningful: Faculty efforts to increase student civic engagement skills. *Transformations: The Journal of Inclusive Scholarship and Pedagogy, xiv*(2), 87–100.

Gelmon, S. B., Agre-Kippenhan, S., & Cress, C. (2005). Beyond a grade: Are we making a difference? In C. M. Cress, P. J. Collier, V. L. Reitenauer, & Associates (Eds.), *Learning through serving: A student guidebook for service-learning across the disciplines* (pp. 125–138). Sterling, VA: Stylus.

Gelmon, S. B., Holland, B. A., Driscoll, A., Spring, A., & Kerrigan, S. (2001). *Assessing service-learning and civic engagement: Principles and techniques.* Providence, RI: Campus Compact.

22

EXPECTING THE POLITICAL, GETTING THE INTERVIEW

How Students (Do Not) See Writing as a Political Act

Catherine Gabor

"What??!!" I thought to myself as several students in my service-learning class confidently asserted that their projects included no *political engagement*. These were students responsible for revising an environmental advocacy website and writing a proposal to the city council to garner acreage for community farming and gardening. How could they possibly fail to see their written work as a form of political engagement?

Rather than casting that question as a failure of the students, though, I quickly turned to examine my own teaching. If I saw their projects as a form of political engagement, and their audiences saw their writing as political advocacy as well, where had I missed the mark in helping the students perceive their own efforts in that manner?

Writing as a Political Act: Course Background

I revamped an existing professional writing course to include an emphasis on teaching for political engagement through service-learning. Students in the course had to produce a significant document for a local agency or organization with a political or policy-making bent. In my class, the writing itself is the service. For example, some student groups produced website copy for the city's newly formed Office of Youth Services or for a local environmental advocacy group; other student groups wrote reports for county agencies responsible for issues ranging from homelessness to immigrants' services. One student group helped a fledgling grassroots organization obtain land for a community farming project, while another produced fund-raising texts for an after-school program for at-risk youth. Each group consisted of three to five students who met regularly during and outside class.

Based on a survey I distributed to the class, several groups of students reported high project and academic success, course satisfaction, and increased efficacy of knowledge and skills. However, a disconcerting and unexpected trend also emerged—many students did not perceive their service-learning for political engagement projects as a political act.

In academic settings students (and often professors) usually view writing as a commodity in exchange for a grade. In contrast, I wanted students to see this Professional Writing course as political action, a model they are not accustomed to in or out of English classes. For example, in most courses that employ service-learning, writing functions as a means for reflecting upon action rather than as action itself. English studies scholar Tom Deans (2000) has categorized this as writing about the community model. Alternatively, writing professors may be in a vanguard position among service-learning practitioners as being most prepared to help students see the act of writing as political engagement.

Because students are so accustomed to divorcing writing from the real world, they may miss the inherent political character of service-learning projects that are based on writing. In response to the question, "What was the last thing you wrote?" students frequently refer to a paper from a previous semester, failing to recognize e-mail messages or other everyday texts as writing. This tendency contributes to the problem of students' seeing their written projects as political action and further prevents their preparation for future political engagement.

Reframing Political Engagement

Often the word *political* alienates and appears disagreeable to students. While many college teachers consider political engagement to be the zenith of democratic ideals, for many students *political* is a bankrupt word and concept. Kiesa et al. (2008) note that millennials—those born between 1985 and

2004—are involved locally with others but are ambivalent about formal politics. If students eschew the very notion of political engagement, then service-learning professors need strategies for meeting students where they are philosophically while still pushing them experientially.

Student Profiles: Andrew and Kristin

"Andrew" and "Kristin" are examples of bright students who resisted seeing their work on the class projects as political engagement. Andrew took the course with me the first time I taught it; Kristin enrolled a year later, after I added a midterm presentation assignment that I hoped would help students define their own work in class projects as political in nature. This new assignment did not work as well as I had planned, but the experience of teaching the class a second time further solidified my contention that students need direct assistance in making the connection between academic experiences and democratic action. Ironically, individual interviews I conducted after the course concluded may have facilitated students' most profound learning insights. Free from the constraints of grades and project timelines, the interviews allowed space for some students to reconsider and finally grasp the political dimensions of their writing.

Andrew

Andrew was one of five students who collaborated on revising website copy for a local environmental group. This community partner wanted the website to be "less wonky" and appeal to average citizens of the region. Each student had two sections of the website to rewrite. In the course of revising the copy, the students looked at other environmental websites, interviewed the community partners, and submitted drafts to the executive director. Their experience was roughly equal to that of their class peers in terms of workload, political focus (at least in my perception), and timeline. However, this group as a whole did not see the project as a form of political engagement.

For example, when I asked whether they learned anything about political engagement from the group project experience, students answered no and said, "Our project was not really political." In comparison, the other groups of students who were writing directly to political audiences such as the mayor's office and the county board of supervisors all consistently responded that their written work was political engagement.

During the course, students in Andrew's group had no problem seeing ordinary people (i.e., readers of the website) as the service beneficiaries of their writing, but these perceptions kept the projects solely within the realm of service-learning and not in the realm of political engagement.

However, at the end of the course when I interviewed students about their experiences, Andrew and his group came to realize that they did know a lot about expressing complicated policy stances in commonsense language for the average citizen. And they began to conceive of that as a political act. In my interview with Andrew, he said,

> Well, reflecting now, I'm thinking that a lot of the writing we're giving to the [web]site is going to be used for a political purpose. So in that sense I suppose we've learned something about political engagement because we've created something that's going to be used for political reasons. Maybe not [for] politicians, but maybe for the average person to understand policies.

Andrew explicitly calls his experience political, not service or community engagement or another safe term—but political. What he reveals is a new perceptual framing of service-learning as political engagement and, by extrapolation, he sees the writing tasks his group conducted as the same kinds of tasks that politically engaged professionals perform.

The interview served as an opportunity for Andrew to reflect upon and make new meaning from his service experience; he now viewed writing as a political act. Concurrently, I realized as an instructor the responsibility (and opportunities) I held for building democratic knowledge bridges.

Kristin

The second time I taught the Professional Writing class, I included a new assignment: a midterm presentation. This assignment would help prepare students for their final presentation, and it would serve as a platform for opening up discussion about the political nature of the projects. Most of the presentations were tentative, but the students did manage to identify some political aspects of their projects. I felt elated as an effective instructor—until I interviewed Kristin at the end of the semester.

Kristin's group was charged with writing a 20-page segment of a larger proposal to the local city council. The group's community partner was a grassroots organization working to secure acreage in the city for community farming and gardening. The community partner had been given half an acre by the city; it was asking for 11 more.

During the end-of-course interviews, all the students in Kristin's group could identify the political nature of their project and describe specific skills and attitudes that could lead them to future political participation. However, when asked if she learned anything about political engagement in general, Kristin replied, "I don't really think so." Furthermore, when I asked, "Did you learn anything specifically about political engagement from writing for and interacting with your community partner?" Kristen stated:

> Political Engagement is a weird term. . . . I don't think I was being politi-
> cally engaged with this project. [Our community partner] is a very political
> organization. They are trying to make change in the community and fight
> for the poor and bring services to people who cannot get them, but my
> experience was just writing something to help them. . . . It wasn't like I
> joined them to do what they are doing. It was like I will do my writing
> task to help you because I think that they are trying to do something good
> for the community.

Kristin resisted labeling her contribution as political in nature and instead characterized it as "just writing," echoing the aforementioned tendency to see writing as bounded by academia. She seemed comfortable acknowledging that her writing task may "do something good for the community," but nothing more.

Political scientist Nicholas Longo (2004) argues that community service for today's student is often not an "alternative to politics," but an "alternative politics," which he calls "service politics" (p. 63). During my interviews, Andrew had a political insight breakthrough; Kristin never quite managed that, acknowledging only that written documents can be used to educate and therefore empower people.

Instructional Insights

Like Andrew, I had my own breakthrough: Interviews can serve as a rich site for generative reflection by students and faculty alike. Without the interviews, I would never have heard what deep and empowering learning can come from intentional education for political engagement. While interviewing students is time-consuming and labor-intensive, it turned out to be the happiest accident of my teaching and scholarly research plan. In the future, I will conduct more end-of-semester interviews to help me gain a deeper understanding of the intersections in writing instruction, service-learning, and political engagement. I will also incorporate guided questioning and more written and oral assignments in class to help students make reflective connections. Finally, I will continue to collect data and assess how professional writing can be taught and experienced as a form of political action.

References

Kiesa, A., Orlowski, A. P., Levine, P., Both, D., Hoban Kirby, E., Hugo Lopez, M., et al. (2008). *Millennials talk politics: A study of college student politics engagement.* College Park, MD: Center for Information & Research on Civic Learning and Engagement.

Deans, T. (2000). *Writing partnerships: Service-learning in composition.* Urbana, IL: National Council of Teachers of English.

Longo, N. V. (2004). The new student politics: Listening to the political voice of students. *Journal of Public Affairs, 7,* 61–74.

23

ADDRESSING POLICY DILEMMAS WITH COMMUNITY-BASED RESEARCH AND ASSESSING STUDENT OUTCOMES

Laura Nichols, Fernando Cázares, and Angelica Rodriguez

Every night individuals without permanent homes ride public transportation all night long for shelter, usually riding the same line over and over again. A problem? A solution? A strategy? A dilemma? It depends on your perspective.

The phenomenon of unhoused people riding the bus for shelter brought many stakeholders together in our county: transportation officials, union representatives, social service providers, police, and city and county staff. While all agreed that the matter was multifaceted and that more information about the unhoused riders was needed, lack of funds in city and county social service programs, limited outreach staff, and uncertainty about who was responsible to act created an impasse among stakeholders. Fernando, who at the time worked for the City of San José's Homeless Services Division, asked Laura if her Applied Sociology class could help fill this information vacuum by doing a community-based research project as described by Strand, Marullo, Cutforth, Stoecker, and Donohue (2003) to find out who the unhoused riders and what their potential needs are. The goal was to have students learn to apply social science research methods to address a community and public policy dilemma and to bring the voices of those left out, the unhoused riders, into policy discussions.

The Class and Project

The Applied Sociology class is a 10-week required course for junior and senior sociology majors to learn how to apply their research skills and find out about career options at the individual, organizational, community, and policy levels. The bus project was one of five community-based research projects offered that term from which students could choose. On the first day of class students ranked their project preferences. Because the project required intensive training before data collection, and students would spend hours at night on the bus, only students who ranked that project as their first choice were selected.

As part of the class students were also required to attend at least one policy meeting. Most attended a meeting of a blue-ribbon commission whose members discussed how to end homelessness in the county within 10 years. Those at the meeting included mayors, housing developers, shelter providers, health care administrators, county officials, the police chief, and other high-ranking officials. Attending this meeting allowed students to hear a variety of perspectives on homelessness in one venue and to compare and contrast competing interests. Students on the bus project also went through specialized training conducted by the transportation authority, which included perspectives from unhoused riders and staff of a local mental health agency (also see Nichols, Cázares, and Rodriguez, in press, for a more in-depth description of the project and the class).

What Riders Shared

The data collected by the students included field notes from observations and recollections of conversations with riders as well as the responses from 49 surveys. The results revealed high usage of the bus for shelter by those surveyed, with some saying that they actively chose the bus over emergency shelters because they saw it as a safer and healthier option. Conversations with riders also revealed the interconnections of community agencies where an action in one area affected other areas. For example, "Patrick" said:

I've been sleeping here [on the bus] for a few months. Before I started sleeping here I would sleep in a park somewhere. They started closing that park down at night, so homeless people cannot sleep there anymore; I had to find a new spot to sleep. I just try to find a place that is safe enough that I won't be accosted. The bus is warm and a safe place to sleep.

Riders talked about how they pieced together a life in libraries, day centers, hospitals, restaurants, hotels, and shelters and described the services and resources they needed (see Nichols and Cázares, in press, for a full discussion of the findings).

The data were analyzed and summarized by the students in a final report and presentation. A two-page research brief was posted on the city of San José's website and has been widely distributed across community agencies. Because the data collection process involved real stories and quotes, stakeholders were able to see unhoused riders as people facing difficult dilemmas each night. In sum, the students' community-based research informed policy makers about the reality of riders' lives, perspectives previously missing from the discussions.

Student Learning Outcomes

While the project and class had an educational impact on the community, it also influenced students. To assess student outcomes, students were given a pre- and posttest that measured political efficacy as well as future career interests, and were asked if they thought they would be civically engaged in the future. Students scored very high in political efficacy on the pretest survey (given on the first day of class prior to the service-learning experience), with over 80% saying they planned to be civically engaged in the future. Despite this, the posttest results showed increases in political efficacy and interest in civic engagement.

In written reflections, students described increased confidence in their individual abilities to enact change: "[I was] greatly influenced by this class and the group project. I feel more confident in myself and my abilities. . . . Working in a group taught me to trust myself and learn how to trust others to collaborate successfully," and "I feel I would do a good job in public office and I feel more strongly that what I do impacts what the government does."

In terms of external efficacy, students said: "Now I feel like public officials do care about what my age group thinks and does and that I can be effective in government," and "I feel I have learned a great deal about public policy and how policies are created. Also, with our speakers, I learned that not all politicians are as bad as we often see them."

Students also remarked on how the project affected their future career aspirations in applying their sociological skills. Said one student, "This class has definitely helped me solidify what I want to pursue as a career and not be afraid to say it," and "This class has helped me understand the opportunities that are out there for sociology majors whether they directly use their sociology degrees or not."

Most striking were the outcomes for the small number of students who in the pretest either said they would not be civically engaged in the future ($n = 4$) or left the question blank ($n = 4$). In the posttest, all these students answered yes to this question, as illustrated by the following: "Originally I put down that I didn't think I would be a civically engaged citizen in the future; but now I do. . . . Also, doing our projects I think I have a better understanding of how I can change policy, whereas before I didn't think so—this makes me feel like I have a say in politics when I didn't before."

Conclusion

This case study provides an opportunity for students to see the dilemmas involved in doing policy work and to see policy makers and politicians as real people trying to balance competing interests and concerns. In terms of community impact, the outcomes are more difficult to identify. The direct result was mainly educational, informing the public and stakeholders about what it is like to ride the bus each night for shelter. The stories from the riders also helped stakeholders move beyond their previous impasse to form positive working relationships and come together over the larger problem of homelessness, rather than just focus on bus riders. And as a result of connections made with city officials, a service-learning opportunity for students to do outreach with people who are unhoused and not using shelters has been created as well as a partnership between university researchers and community service providers who want more community-based assessment. To date, policies to restrict the ability of unhoused riders to use the bus for shelter have not been developed. It is unclear if this is the result of stakeholders' better understanding of the situations of unhoused riders or simply a consequence of budgets and other more pressing issues.

The skills and resources in universities and among students provide a means for communities to gain a fuller understanding of policy dilemmas by learning from people like the unhoused riders who may be most affected by policy changes but are least likely to have a voice in the analysis or response. In this way the university can play an important role in helping undo the oversimplification of issues found in the media and among some policy makers to help the public better understand the often complicated nature of community issues. And such pedagogy allows students to engage in real dilemmas, with murky solutions, to more fully appreciate the constraints and pressures faced by people without homes, policy makers, and service providers while adding previously missing information and voices to the discussion.

References

Nichols, L., & Cázares, F. (in press). Homelessness and the mobile shelter system: Public transportation as shelter. *Journal of Social Policy, 40*(3).

Nichols, L., Cázares, F., & Rodriguez, A. (in press). Educating about homelessness: A university-city government research partnership. In P. Nyden, L. Hossfeld, & G. Nyden (Eds.), *Public sociology: Research, action, and change*. Thousand Oaks, CA: Sage.

Strand, K., Marullo, S., Cutforth, N., Stoecker, R., & Donohue, P. (2003). *Community-based research and higher education*. San Francisco, CA: Jossey-Bass.

24

SERVICE-LEARNING FOR A DEMOCRATIC FUTURE

David M. Donahue and Christine M. Cress

olleges and universities have long claimed for themselves a role in the education and preparation of young people for democratic participation. Indeed, Leal Filho (2002) asserts that the success of a postsecondary institution should be judged by its ability to educate students for globally informed and democratically responsible leadership. Just as Dewey (1916/1961) asserted that education should not be merely the "subject matter of the schools, isolated from the subject matter of life experience" (pp. 10–11), Jickling (2004) argues that a sustainable future is dependent upon students fully engaging their knowledge, skills, and attitudes in collaboratively judging the "relative merits of contenting possibilities" (p. 137) in addressing the needs of communities.

Producing civic-minded graduates who possess problem-solving and democratic leadership abilities requires institutional and individual instructor intentionality. But many faculty, especially those outside academic disciplines that explicitly address politics, have often been unclear and conflicted about how to accomplish this goal. Similarly, service-learning faculty have been unclear and conflicted about instructional approaches. In fact, as the contributors to this book openly describe, service-learning faculty may face even more ambiguity and conflict as they negotiate the democratic dilemmas inherent in service-learning:

- What if a student's idea for a service-learning project is antithetical to a faculty member's ideas of participation in a democratic society?

- What if students in a classroom find it difficult to accommodate an unpopular point of view or one artlessly expressed?
- What if students propose service in the form of educating citizens but find no one willing to be a learning participant?

Yet as the authors have explicated, these dilemmas are not obstacles to preparing students for political engagement but are the very curriculum for developing such engagement. Such an understanding that dilemmas are the text for learning rather than obstacles to it is perhaps one of the greatest democratic opportunities provided by service-learning. Acknowledging these dilemmas broadens our understanding of how to teach for civic engagement. And by sharing these dilemmas with others in our academic professions, we expand the community of scholars conducting civically engaged teaching and community-based scholarship.

To achieve these valued outcomes from service-learning, faculty must be deliberate in course design, teaching and learning processes, and assessment activities. If students are to learn academic content from service, faculty need to provide opportunities for students to reflect on those connections. Experience alone is not enough.

In addition, students need practice in recognizing and resolving dilemmas. As described by Cuban (2001), dilemmas are tensions that lead to intractable situations because of conflicting value perspectives. Dilemmas stand in contrast to problems that are often technical in nature. So, for example, different expectations and understandings by faculty, students, and community partners of service-learning outcomes require open communication that can be facilitated by putting expectations in writing, raising and making explicit assumptions that each party brings to the service experience, and avoiding jargon or language accessible only to those on the same side. In sum, to promote civic engagement, faculty must provide students with opportunities to learn the knowledge, skills, and dispositions necessary to participate in democratic life.

Next Step: Create a Scholarly Community

This text evolved directly from a community of scholars brought together by California Campus Compact and the Carnegie Foundation for the Advancement of Teaching and Learning to facilitate service-learning for political engagement. Just as the Fellows discovered that service-learning for political engagement raised practical and theoretical dilemmas, we found that bringing together and facilitating a scholarly community raises its own set of dilemmas:

- Should the community be open to anyone interested regardless of experience with service-learning?
- How do we draw on the diverse experiences and backgrounds of the faculty?
- How do we collaborate when individuals operate with different definitions of what is democratic citizenship?
- As student learning is developmental and socially constructed, how can faculty learning and professional development be effectively facilitated?

Many colleges and universities have teaching excellence centers or offices for community service-learning. The professionals who direct these offices frequently offer brown-bag lunch discussions, workshops, and professional learning communities for integrating service-learning into teaching and scholarship. Check to see what infrastructure and resource support may exist on your own campus and how they may be addressing these questions. Also, find out if your state has a Campus Compact affiliation office, because this can be another source for grants, trainings, and other professional development opportunities. In addition, the National Service-Learning Clearinghouse website (http://www.servicelearning.org/) contains multiple service-learning syllabus examples, reflection practices, and research-based articles on how to teach and assess service-learning. Finally, find like-minded colleagues with whom you can share your own dilemmas and strategies for teaching service-learning. Certainly, any of the contributors to this volume would be willing to further provide ideas for successful teaching either via electronic means or through a campus visit. (For author contact information see the Contributor section beginning on p. 195.)

As Banks (2008) states, a fundamental purpose of education is to improve the human condition. Will a single service-learning course ameliorate suffering or rectify injustices? Of course not. But service-learning is an optimal environment for connecting academic knowledge and skills with democratic challenges and hopes. Parks (2000) describes this kind of critical consciousness as a distinctive mode of making meaning where students "become critically aware of one's own composing of reality" (p. 6). When we delve boldly into the dilemmas of democracy and provide students with the tools and practical experience for applying their knowledge and skills to the community through service-learning, we actively participate in the creation of a democratically educated and civically engaged future.

References

Banks, J. A. (2008). Diversity, group identity, and citizenship education in a global age. *Educational Researcher, 37*(3), 129–139.

Cuban, L. (2001). *How can I fix it? Finding solutions and managing dilemmas.* New York, NY: Teachers College Press.

Dewey, J. (1961). *Democracy and education: An introduction to the philosophy of education.* New York, NY: Macmillan. (Original work published 1916)

Jickling, B. (2004). Why I don't want my children educated for sustainable development. In W. Scott & S. Gough (Eds.), *Key issues in sustainable development and learning* (pp. 133–137). New York, NY: RoutledgeFalmer.

Leal Filho, W. L. (2002). *Teaching sustainability in universities: Towards curriculum greening.* New York, NY: Peter Lang.

Parks, S. D. (2000). *Big questions, worthy dreams: Mentoring young adults in their search for meaning, purpose, and faith.* San Francisco, CA: Jossey-Bass.

CONTRIBUTORS

RaeLyn Axlund, research and assessment director, Washington Campus Compact, raelyn.axlund@wwu.edu

Lynne A. Bercaw, associate professor, education, California State University, Chico, lbercaw@csuchico.edu

Becky Boesch, assistant professor, educational leadership and policy, Portland State University, boeschb@pdx.edu

Christopher Brooks, associate dean for sciences, associate professor, computer science, University of San Francisco, cbrooks@usfca.edu

Fernando Cázares, formerly development specialist at Homeless Services Division, City of San José, CA, cazares_fernando@hotmail.com

Corey Cook, assistant professor, assistant director, politics, and director, Leo T. McCarthy Center for Public Service and the Common Good, University of San Francisco, cdcook2@usfca.edu

Christine M. Cress, professor, Postsecondary, Adult, and Continuing Education (PACE) Program, Portland State University, cressc@pdx.edu

David M. Donahue, associate professor, education, Mills College, ddonahue @mills.edu

Molli K. Fleming, associate professor, Spanish, service-learning coordinator, University of Hawaii Maui College, mollif@hawaii.edu

Catherine Gabor, assistant professor, writing program director, English and comparative literature, San José State University, catherine.gabor@sjsu.edu

Katja M. Guenther, assistant professor, sociology, University of California, Riverside, katja@ucr.edu

Caroline Heldman, associate professor, politics, Occidental College, heldman @oxy.edu

Marcia Hernandez, assistant professor, sociology, University of the Pacific, mhernandez@pacific.edu

Judith Liu, professor, sociology, University of San Diego, liuusd @SanDiego.edu

Laura Nichols, associate professor, sociology, Santa Clara University, LNichols@scu.edu

Tanya Renner, professor of psychology, social sciences department, Kapiʻolani Community College, renner@hawaii.edu

Angelica Rodriguez, MPH candidate, program in health and social behavior, University of California Berkeley, florecitaxicana@yahoo.com

Sandra A. Sgoutas-Emch, professor, psychological sciences, University of San Diego, emch@sandiego.edu

Stephanie Stokamer, senior instructor, Postsecondary, Adult, and Continuing Education (PACE) Program, Portland State University, stokamer @pdx.edu

Dari E. Sylvester, assistant professor, political science, and senior fellow, Harold S. Jacoby Center for Public Service and Civic Leadership, University of the Pacific, dsylvester@pacific.edu

Lucero Topete, director of Instituto Cultural Oaxaca, México, info@ icomexico.com

Thomas J. Van Cleave, doctoral student, postsecondary education, Portland State University, tjv@pdx.edu

Kathleen S. Yep, associate professor, Asian American studies, Pitzer College, kathleen_yep@pitzer.edu

Encountering Faith in the Classroom
Turning Difficult Discussions into Constructive Engagement
Edited by Miriam R. Diamond
Foreword by Art Chickering

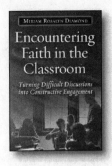

"In this book, religion and spirituality are not explored in terms of coercing or changing one's belief system nor is this book an effort to espouse which, if any, religion is correct. Instead, it is about learning and better understanding one's own religion or lack thereof, as well as the religious convictions of others. Further, it is about being able to have dialogue around these topics which are great influences on who we are."—*Education Review*

22883 Quicksilver Drive
Sterling, VA 20166-2102

Subscribe to our e-mail alerts: www.Styluspub.com

Also available from Stylus

Learning through Serving
A Student Guidebook for Service-Learning Across the Disciplines
Christine M. Cress, Peter J. Collier and Vicki L. Reitenauer

"[This] is a self-directed guide for college students engaged in service-learning. The purpose of the book is to walk the reader through elements of learning and serving by focusing on how students can 'best provide meaningful service to a community agency or organization while simultaneously gaining new skills, knowledge, and understanding as an integrated aspect of the [student's] academic program.' Intended as a textbook, this work reads like a conversation between the authors and the college student learner. The publication is student-friendly, comprehensive, easy to follow, and full of helpful activities."—*Journal of College Student Development*

"Learning Through Serving could be easily adapted to any current service course or to supply the framework for developing a new course. It is thoughtful and useful for instructors and students . . . Institutions that desire their graduates learn to be the catalysts of change the world needs, should not overlook this useful and inspiring work."—*Teaching Theology and Religion*

Service Learning for Civic Engagement Series
Series Editor: Gerald Eisman

Each volume in this series is organized around a specific community issue—social justice, gender inequity, community health, political engagement—and provides multiple perspectives on both the theoretical foundations for understanding the issues, and purposeful approaches to addressing them. The monographs are suitable for interdisciplinary studies, faculty, and student learning circles, thematic course clusters, and other forms of integrative learning where service learning is a primary method of delivery. The articles in each monograph provide a panoply of exemplary practices, insights, and course materials to enhance civic learning.

Available:

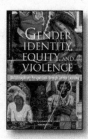   

Gender Identity, Equity, and Violence
Edited by Geraldine B. Stahly

Promoting Health and Wellness in Underserved Communities
Edited by Anabel Pelham and Elizabeth Sills

Race, Poverty, and Social Justice
Edited by José Calderón

Research, Advocacy, and Political Engagement
Edited by Sally Tannenbaum